25 Plays from The Fire This Time Festival

25 Plays from The Fire This Time Festival

A DECADE OF RECOGNITION, RESISTANCE, RESILIENCE, REBIRTH, AND BLACK THEATER

Edited by
KELLEY NICOLE GIROD

methuen | drama
LONDON • NEW YORK • OXFORD • NEW DELHI • SYDNEY

METHUEN DRAMA
Bloomsbury Publishing Plc
50 Bedford Square, London, WC1B 3DP, UK
1385 Broadway, New York, NY 10018, USA
29 Earlsfort Terrace, Dublin 2, Ireland

BLOOMSBURY, METHUEN DRAMA and the Methuen Drama logo are trademarks of
Bloomsbury Publishing Plc

First published in Great Britain 2022
Introduction and Foreword Copyright © Kelley Nicole Girod, 2022

For individual play and foreword copyrights, please see Permissions and Acknowledgements on p. 189.

A catalogue record for this book is available from the British Library.

A catalog record for this book is available from the Library of Congress.

ISBN: HB: 978-1-3502-6811-1
        PB: 978-1-3502-6810-4
        ePDF: 978-1-3502-6812-8
        eBook: 978-1-3502-6813-5

Typeset by RefineCatch Limited, Bungay, Suffolk
Printed and bound in Great Britain

To find out more about our authors and books visit www.bloomsbury.com
and sign up for our newsletters.

Dedications and Thanks

This book is dedicated to playwright Christine Jean Chambers (9/8/1980–12/4/2019), The Fire This Time Season 2 playwright, festival photographer, and dear community member, and Sidiki Fofana (7/28/89–7/20/17), The Fire This Time Season 8 actor and beloved community member

Special thanks to Kim Weild, Nicole A. Watson, Dennis A. Allen II, Tonya Pinkins, Jonathan McCrory, and Abigail Katz

Acknowledgments to festival co-founders Germono Toussaint and Derek Lee McPhatter, Zach Woolford, and former Artistic Director Kevin R. Free

Contents

I. A History of The Fire This Time Festival

The title of African American playwright, novelist, activist, and icon James Baldwin's book *The Fire Next Time* was taken from a line of the negro spiritual "Mary Don't You Weep" which states, "God gave Noah the rainbow sign, no more water, the fire next time." Baldwin's influential book about race relations in the 1960s pays homage to the African American legacy and responds to our ancestors' calls to each generation to take up the torch passed that will continue to lead us further into the future. It was with this in mind that The Fire This Time Festival was founded over a decade ago. In 2009 seven Black playwrights came together in a tiny East Village theater to discuss the state of Black theatermakers in an industry that was not changing as quickly as the world around it. What came out of that discussion was a weekend presentation of ten-minute plays by Black playwrights that immediately sold out. Over ten years later, The Fire This Time Festival now consists of two weeks of programming including the flagship ten-minute showcase, full-length readings, a new works lab, panel discussions, and year-round programming that now features digital collaborations.

While The Fire This Time Festival's main goal has been to amplify the voices of Black playwrights and storytellers, we also seek to show the vast spectrum of Blackness, and move beyond common ideas of what's possible in Black theater, a benchmark that has too long been dictated by the overwhelming white gaze of American theater. For this reason, selected playwrights are not given a theme to write on. Every playwright is simply encouraged to showcase their unique voice. The Fire This Time's motto is "any play written by a Black playwright is a Black expression even if it is about two white people in love." By allowing our artists this freedom of expression, The Fire This Time has become known as a space where Black exploration on stage is not only diverse, but exhilarating. Over the years plays have ranged in style from straight dramas to avant garde to poetic including adaptations of British classics, to sci-fi pieces, comedies, dramadies, family plays, and one-person shows. Furthermore, the plays have addressed a vast swatch of themes over the years, and in a time of incredible racial and cultural tension in America, the playwrights have tackled police brutality, institutional racism, homophobia, the Black Lives Matter movement, and the effect that slavery still has in our country.

Completing its eleventh season in 2020, the Festival has presented new work from over seventy Black playwrights and hundreds of collaborating directors, performers, and other theater professionals.

In 2014, The Fire This Time launched its first touring production, bringing its programming to audiences in Boston. In 2015 the festival received its first Obie Award in recognition of outstanding achievement. In 2021, the Festival received a prestigious two-year funding grant from The Black Seed. The Festival has nurtured the development of countless new works, leading to alumni playwright opportunities at the Public Theater, the Atlantic Theater Company, Steppenwolf Theater Company, Lincoln Center Theater, NYTW, and MCC among others. Other writers have gone on to success in features, television, music, web-series, and other arts and entertainment platforms.

The fire next time is The Fire This Time.

The Playwrights

2010 Season 1

Deborah Asiimwe, Radha Blank, Kelley Nicole Girod, Katori Hall, Germono Toussaint, Derek Lee McPhatter, Pia Wilson

2011 Season 2

Jesse Cameron Alick, Christine Jean Chambers, Camille Darby, Marcus Gardley, Yusef Miller, Dominique Morisseau

2012 Season 3

France-Luce Benson, Jocelyn Bioh, Kevin R. Free, Patricia Ione Lloyd, Zoey Martinson, Antoinette Nwandu, Jerome A. Parker

2013 Season 4

Dennis A. Allen II, Danielle Davenport, Jason Holtham, Eric Lockley, Cynthia Robinson, Tracey Conyer Lee, Nathan Yungerburg

2014 Season 5

Erica Rose, Angelica Cheri, Josh Wilder, Lori Parquet, Judy Tate, Jonathan Payne

2015 Season 6

Aziza Barnes, Roderick Gailes OBC, Julienne Hairston, Azure D. Osborne-Lee, Larry Powell, James Anthony Tyler, Daaimah Mubashshir

2016 Season 7

Tanya Everett, Keelay Gipson, Mansa Ra (formerly known as Jireh Breon Holder), Roger Q. Mason, Stacey Rose, Nia Witherspoon, Korde Tuttle; season directed by Nicole A, Watson

2017 Season 8

Karen Chilton, Jordan E. Cooper, Shamar S. White, Michelle Tyrene Johnson, Eliana Pipes, Fredrica Bailey, C.A. Johnson; season directed by Cezar Williams

2018 Season 9

Sandra A. Daley-Sharif, Shelley Fort, Gethsemane Herron-Coward, Charly Evon Simpson, Mona R. Washington, William Oliver Watkins; season directed by Candis C. Jones

2019 Season 10

Kendra Augustin, Francisca Da Silvera, Adrienne Dawes, Samantha Godfrey, Garlia Cornelia Jones, Bernard Tarver, York Walker, Kezia Waters; season directed by Kevin R. Free

2020 Season 11

Cyrus Aaron, Niccolo Aeed, Natyna Bean, Tyler English-Beckwith, Jay Mazcyk, Deneen Reynolds-Knott, Mario (Mars) Wolfe; season directed by Ebony Noelle Golden

II. Foreword: The Privilege of Identity and Why I Founded The Fire This Time Festival

"What are you?" By the time I was seven I learned to anticipate this question from strangers, from potential new friends, and even from teachers. And at such a young age I knew it was not a question being asked to understand where my almond eyes, bent nose, curly black hair, and light skin came from. In the majority white world where my features stood out, "What are you?" was an attempt to collect data that would determine what the dynamic would be in a relationship, what should and should not be said around me, and ultimately to remind me of my place in an unspoken caste system. Growing up Black/mixed descent in America, "What are you" is a question that came to define my existence, further complicated by a country that excelled at erasing the roots of those they enslaved. I was told I was Black, but had no sense of the ancestors who gave me my curly roots or distinct nose. I only now know of my ancestry from Nigeria, Cameroon, Congo, Western Bantu, and Mali, but these ancestors still remain nameless and faceless. On the other hand, my European ancestry going back to France, then Nova Scotia, then Acadiana where my ancestors founded the first Cajun settlement and gave my parents the Cajun/Creole French tongue they spoke in childhood was well documented. I remember the pride I felt the first time I saw my Cajun ancestors' names on plaques in a museum in the central square of the town that they founded, St. Martinville. Near the museum was a tree by the Bayou Teche marked for the fictional Evangeline and Gabriel in Henry Wadsworth Longfellow's famous and epic poem *Evangeline: A Tale of Acadie*, a poem I still love. I suddenly saw myself in Wadsworth's words, a tangible connection to my past and present. And in that moment I realized the power of identity. The currency of identity. The luxury of identity. The confidence that knowing who you are affords one. And ultimately, the role of storytelling in establishing and maintaining identity. And my deepest desire in that moment was to solidify my identity, to be someone who was no longer crushed by the dehumanizing question of "What are you?", nor defined by it. It was this desire that led me to storytelling and storytelling led me to The Fire This Time Festival.

By the time I left graduate school I had already decided that my stories being boxed into a neat definition of what was considered Black art by white standards was non-negotiable. If anything had helped me exorcise the ghosts of "What are you?" it was my writing which brought me to my darkest edges and back and gave me a hard-won identity I was beginning to stand firm in. The other side of the coin of beginning to find myself was the desire to find my community. There were other exciting young Black playwrights I had been hearing about and I was desperate to know them. That yearning led to an email, then to a meeting where we playwrights huddled in a circle in a tiny East Village theater. That day The Fire This Time Festival was born, a movement was set in motion, and a community that continually contributed beautiful brushstrokes on the vast, ever evolving landscape of Blackness, Black art, and Black expression came into being.

"What are you?" I now know that part of that answer lies in the twenty-five plays contained in this collection, in places where my Blackness overlaps with the experiences of my fellow Black playwrights, places where, until I witnessed their stories on stage, I was told Blackness could not exist. I am my community, ever expanding, without boundaries, limitless. I am Black. I am The Fire This Time Festival.

III. Play Sections

Section 1

Vanna White, Brooke Shields, and Beyoncé: Beauty Standards and Self-Acceptance in Black America

Since its founding, the US has employed caricatured images of people of color as lazy, violent, dangerous, dirty, and uneducated, among others, to maintain a servant class. These images persisted long after the emancipation and morphed into the subconscious of generations of Americans. The image of the Black woman was doubly assaulted: not only was she everything listed above, but her beautiful fullness, deep brown skin, and soft curly hair were flagged by white society as markers of sexual immorality and the very embodiment of "ugly." Moreover, being Black and LGBTQ was never acknowledged as anything more than an abomination. A cishet, eurocentric ideal of beauty has flourished in America and still holds much of the real estate in print and media. But in the past decade candid conversations around colorism and inclusivity have started the process of not only mainstream media's need to look at its standards of beauty and expand their definitions, it has led to a reclaiming of Black as beautiful amongst Blacks as seen in such events as the natural hair movement among others. In this section, Katori Hall's *The Beyoncé Effect*, Antoinette Nwandu's *Vanna White Has Got to Die!*, Roger Q. Mason's *Hard Palate*, and Derek Lee McPhatter's *Citizen Jane*, we see the effects of history's various stereotyping of Blacks, as well the persistent prominence of whiteness and the white gaze on how Blacks and people of color are seen and see themselves. Furthermore, these plays also show us how the white gaze can even affect the Black psyche, manifesting itself in a voice that consistently disrupts and sabotages. And ultimately and most importantly, these plays beautifully dramatize how we Blacks fight the voices of descent within to claim our own definition of beauty and self-acceptance.

Foreword by Jocelyn Bioh, The Fire This Time Season 3 playwright and writer of the critically acclaimed, award-winning play *School Girls; or, The African Mean Girls Play* which addresses colorism and beauty standards in African, African American, and Black communities

The beauty of the Black body in history is one that the Western world has been confounded by. For most of history, our hues were used as currency. In the case of Sarah Baartman, known to the world as "Venus Hottentot," her body was put on display like a circus act. People would come from miles away and pay money to see her voluptuous derrière. In the case of mixed-race slaves, their currency was their lighter skin—the only reprieve they had from being overworked in the fields—as they were considered more "acceptable" to be in the house. The filtered-down version of all of these ideas and characterizations of the Black body have morphed into new beauty standards in the present day, but for non-Blacks. What was once ridiculed and ogled is now the latest craze in cosmetic surgery with a curvier figure, fuller lips, and tanned skin becoming the gold standard of beauty in America, creating a unique assault on the

Black identity through unapologetic appropriation of features that Blacks have been encouraged to alter in the name of social mobility. The incredible playwrights featured in this section have illustrated how the white gaze seeks to dominate the narratives in what is reflected in Black mirrors, and while overcoming those narratives is not easy, it is not impossible.

Play #1: The Beyoncé Effect *by Katori Hall*

Three brown women struggle with their quest for lighter skin and European features in a world where "if you white, you right, and if you black, get back."

Presented in The Fire This Time Festival Season 1, directed by Martin Damien Wilkins, performed by Vella Lovell, Maechi Aharanwu, and Frances Uku.

Characters

Fury #1
Fury #2
Fury #3

The Beyoncé Effect *by Katori Hall*

The three **Furies** *stand in separate pools of light.*

Fury #1, *a young beautiful South Indian woman, wears a long silk sari, with jasmine falling like ropes from her hair.*

Fury #2, *a young beautiful African woman, wears a vibrant cloth around her hips and the skin on her face is discolored; she is the darkest.*

Fury #3, *a young African American woman, wears her yeast infection jeans and her House of Deréon hoodie—pure Harlem girl she is.*

They are all beautifully chocolate, caramel shades.

Fury #1   Mirror, mirror, on the wall.

Fury #2   Who's the / fairest.

Fury #3   Fairest.

Fury #1 and Fury #3   Of them all?

Fury #3   Not me.

Fury #2   Not me.

Fury #1   Not me.

All   Not me.

They all open a can of skin lightener and begin to smear it across their faces.

Fury #1   Mirror, mirror, on the wall.

Fury #2   Who's the / fairest.

Fury #3   Fairest.

Fury #1 and Fury #3   Of them all?

Fury #3   Not me.

Fury #2   Not me.

Fury #1   Not me.

All   Not me.

Fury #1 and Fury #2 *sit on big blocks as if they are sitting on the shoulders of* **Fury #3**. *They place their hands on her shoulders.*

Fury #3   At first it was for the spots. You know? The little dark spots you get when a bump come up on you too strong. That's all I did it for. I had looked on the internet and saw it was good, it was all good. Go to the beauty supply and cop you a tube of Ambi. Put it on that spot and then BWAM. You'd be back to yo old chocolate glow. You know, though? But—But then the bumps start coming. Coming on strong. By the end of junior high made a bitch look like she had.

Fury #2   Chicken pox.

Fury #1   Measles.

All   Mumps and rubella.

Fury #3   Couldn't even barely hold up my face no more. So heavy from the weight of them dots it was. That's when I started to pick. Pick at them scabs hoping scratchin' at em like lotto tickets hoping that I'd win to find reveal beautiful skin beneath. But every time I removed one dot another one'd pop up in its place. Bigger. Badder.

All   Darker.

Fury #3   It'd get darker. Every spot a recollection of my constant imperfection though I was on a pursuit to perfection. My skin couldn't be smooth. Wouldn't just get smooth.

Fury #1   Smooth.

Fury #2   Smooth.

Fury #3   Smooth like that train ride when you sippin on sysyzurp. Smooth like the flan from your best friend auntie's aluminum pan at the quinciara.

Fury #1   Smooth like the skin of Aishwarya Rai.

Fury #2   Smooth like the skin of the Ethiopian women.

Fury #1 and Fury #3   Flawless.

Fury #3   So yeah, that's why I bought it. Yeah 2 percent hydroquinone to make these spots get gone. Every night. I put on my creams to brighten my battle with the pestilence of adolescence. Some say perm is the creamy crack, but when yo face come under attack Ambi is your drug of choice. Over the counter at that. It first started with the.

Fury #1   Dot dot dot dot dot. (*Like a commercial*) Get your skin clear. Make your skin brighter. Try Triluma Cream, Illuminate the beauty in you.

Fury #2 (*like a commercial*)   Hate those stubborn spots. Try Meladerma. Smooth you to a Lighter, Brighter, Happier hue—I mean you.

Fury #3   But them dots wouldn't go away. I couldn't keep them at bay. Black holes sucking away the star light from my Milky Way complexion, mountains of darkness.

Fury #2 (*sings*)   But you are beautiful / no matter what they say . . .

Fury #3   But the spots started getting / bigger and bigger and bigger.

Fury #1   And the dots started getting / bigger and bigger and bigger.

Fury #2 (*sings*)   But you are beautiful / no matter what they say.

Fury #3   Til my whole face was covered with the creamy crack.

Fury #1   The creamy crack.

Fury #2 (*moaning*)

Fury #3   Til my whole face started disappearing.

Fury #2 (*moaning*)

Fury #1   So beautiful.

Fury #2 (*moaning*)

Fury #1   Disappear the ugly.

Fury #3   And my whole face started fading away. No longer the color of the Milky Way. As days grew past another color replaced my dark pigmentation.

Fury #1   You look so pretty.

Fury #3   Ashen.

Fury #2 (*moaning*)

Fury #3   A light gray.

Fury #1   Stunning. Absolutely stunning you are.

Fury #2 (*moaning*)

Fury #3   Spreading across my face.

Fury #1   A stunnah.

Fury #3   Making that mocha choca latte yah.

Fury #1   You look pretty—

Fury #2   Pretty.

Fury #1 and Fury #2   GONE.

Fury #3   They said with the hands of Whoopi Goldberg and the face of Beyoncé.

Fury #1 and Fury #2 (*cackling like little bitches*)

Fury #3   I took it as a compliment.

All   A compliment.

Fury #3   Because at least for once I had a pretty face.

Fury #2 (*moaning a song beneath it*)

Fury #1   My parents are looking for me a husband. I much rather stay at home. Write. Read. Do anything, but fry another fucking veggie samosa for my father. I, of course, do not speak this. Do not dare say this out loud. To speak here is to have your heart known and woman cannot speak her heart here not matter how loud it is. It makes the world crumble.

Fury #2   Crumble.

Fury #1   "It is time that you are married my daughter. You are so old." My mother says this to my twenty-year-old self. "So unfortunate your age, but at least you went to school, you are prepared to give your husband good conversation." I'm surprised she did not say good head as well. For my heart will be on its knees in no time. They scour the internet for a possible suitor.

Fury #3   No luck there.

Fury #2   Unh, unh. Too ugly.

Fury #3   He ain't got no degree.

Fury #2   His parents are linked to the Bollywood mafia.

Fury #3   Oooooo, what about this one?

Fury #2   Ugh, he has to get his back threaded. Do you want your children to look like werewolves?

Fury #1   This is when they place an ad in the *Hindi Times*. "Proud parents looking for attractive suitor for daughter, Must have MBA or engineering degree, good disposition, Brahmin class. Daughter is a good cook, educated, and fair skin."

"—But mother I am not fair I am—"

Fury #3   Wheat colored. I know. But we have time. It'll take us at least a month to finish all the interviews in the meantime.

Fury #2   She handed me.

All   The jar.

Fury #3   Slather it on three times a day.

Fury #2   Fair and lovely cream.

She raises the tube.

Fury #1   Three times a day.

Fury #2   Three times a day and it is guaranteed.

Fury #2   You won't be.

All   Wheat-colored anymore.

Fury #3   Maybe you'll become pretty.

Fury #1   My mother says, "It is the only way to get a Brahmin man. What a shame that you were cursed with skin the color of caramel but blessed with Aishwarya Rai eyes."

They do their ritual again.

Fury #1   Mirror, mirror, on the wall.

Fury #2   Who's the / fairest.

Fury #3   Fairest.

Fury #1 and Fury #3   Of them all?

Fury #3   Not me.

Fury #2   Not me.

Fury #1   Not me.

All   Not me.

Fury #2   I ordered the tube off of the internet. Fair and lovely cream.

All   The power of beauty.

Fury #2   Said the box crushed by its journey from overseas. I had saved up many shillings for this. My sister called me.

Fury #3   Foolish,

Fury #1   Stupid.

Fury #2   But she was not ugly like me. My sister was blessed. She looked like an Ethiopian queen and a Bugandan king's dream.

Fury #3   Coffee with a lot of milk.

Fury #1   Tea with a lot of sugar.

Fury #2   She looked like the Black women in America whose skin had been tainted by the white man. Cotton-pickers' skin.

Fury #3   So soft with that one drop of / white.

Fury #1   White.

Fury #3   She was called the Beyoncé of Africa.

Fury #1   The Halle of the Hills.

Fury #2   Wanted all over the village. Wanted by my own husband. I saw how he looked at her around the fire at night. Its flicker danced luminous off her skin. Like how fire dances with itself in water's reflection not caring that it can be extinguished. Her beauty loomed bright as embers took flight into the stars. My husband could not take his eyes of my sister.

Fury #1 and Fury #3   My sister.

Fury #2   She was so beautiful.

Fury #1 and Fury #2   My sister.

Fury #2   Who could not not see her? Love her from around that fireside. He could not see me because I disappeared myself. Closing my eyes to stop my whites from announcing my presence. I sat there around that fire hoping to / disappear.

Fury #1 and Fury #2   Disappear into the myself.

Fury #3   And when I opened them they were gone. And I knew.

Fury #1 and Fury #2   Knew.

Silence.

Fury #3   I heard them. In the hut. Vibrating with their passion. I never asked him why. I never asked her. But in two months' time. Just like the box says. I will be fair and lovely like my sister the Beyoncé of Africa.

The women scoop the cream and apply it on their faces. Looking in their mirrors. They do their nightly ritual.

Fury #1   Mirror, mirror, on the wall.

Fury #2   Who's the / fairest.

Fury #3   Fairest.

Fury #1 and Fury #3   Of them all?

Fury #3   Not me.

Fury #2   Not me.

Fury #1   Not me.

All   Not me.

*The spotlight on the **Furies** slowly fades as they scoop beauty from their jars.*

Fury #1   Mirror, mirror, on the wall.

Fury #2   Who's the / fairest.

Fury #3   Fairest.

Fury #1 and Fury #3   Of them all?

Fury #3   Not me.

Fury #2   Not me.

Fury #1   Not me.

All   Not me.

The lights have faded.

Play #2: Citizen Jane *by Derek Lee McPhatter*

The world's favorite superhero comes to life tonight. Don't worry if she seems tired of saving the world. She better give us the happy endings we deserve, or else!

Presented in The Fire This Time Festival Season 1, directed by Rhonney Greene, performed by Lauren Rhodes Cooper (**Citizen Jane**), Dylan Krammerer (**Jess**), LaJune (**Patterson**), Sheree Renee Thomas (**Bot One**), Darren Mallett (**Bot Two**), Nicole Judd (*Stage Manager*).

Characters

Jesse Jackson Jameson, *the architect of today's exhibition. An artist of virtual worlds, Jesse is a cross between a video-game designer and a sculptor. This retrospective is Jesse's most ambitious project.*
Citizen Jane, *a statuesque and practically divine superwoman. Citizen Jane is the heroine and subject of the retrospective. An understated in-person demeanor balances her over-the-top public persona.*
Ro Patterson, *third generation. Spokesperson and Junior Member of the Council on Historical Integrity. Patterson is the grand, exuberant motormouth producer of today's event.*
Bots, *one or more swing players—cyborg assistants who help render various scenes as the play unfolds. Bots also perform various non-speaking side/background characters at the director's discretion.*

Scene

The Museum of Honors—a virtual museum, rendered in 3-D on a futuristic super-network. Today the museum presents a special retrospective.

Time

The distant future.

Notes

1. These characters live in the future, beyond our current ideas of race, gender identity, and so forth. Casting with regards to ethnicity and sex is at the director's discretion. I strongly suggest casting from different ethnic/cultural groups to reflect an integrated future.

2. This play works best at a fast pace, particularly the action sequences.

Citizen Jane *by Derek Lee McPhatter*

Lights up dimly on **Jesse** *at the edge of the empty stage. Open, dark, and free. It terrifies him.*

He looks down at a power cord/plug and follows it offstage.

Something plugs in. Lights up as the network activates! Podiums rise on either side of the stage.

Patterson *appears as* **Jesse** *re-enters.*

Citizen Jane *wanders in, a little grumpy, as if she just woke up.*

Jane*'s gaze falls to* **Jesse** *who has been staring in awe.*

Jane (*to* **Jesse**)   This is the last time.

Patterson   What was that? Jesse?

Citizen Jane *wanders off, heading backstage.*

Patterson   Jesse?

Jesse *looks off after* **Jane***.*

Jesse   I never thought . . .

Patterson   Well, you are an artist. Surely you must think a little. But yes I understand, you . . . emote. You experience. You simply "are." We didn't expect much thinking out of you.

Jesse   That's not what I meant.

Patterson   Never mind all that, Jesse. Today we celebrate.

Jesse   Celebrate.

Patterson   Our audience awaits.

He is suddenly exuberant, looking to the audience.

And you are here! Let us have applause in celebration of the grand occasion!!

The audience applauds. **Patterson** *descends from the podium to continue the introduction.*

Patterson   Welcome!

Jesse   Welcome.

Patterson   My name is Ro Patterson—third generation—and on behalf of the Council on Historic Integrity I greet you with glad tidings and pleasurable salutations, indeed!

Jesse   Indeed, pleasurable salutations and glad tidings to all. My name is Jesse Jackson Jameson and it is truly an honor among honors to be with you this evening!

Patterson   Yes, Jesse Jenkins Johnson, archival architect extraordinaire. We are gathered to celebrate our champion of liberty, freedom, honor, and justice across the ages: Citizen Jane!

He waits for the audience to applaud. Their applause is not satisfactory. He orders the **Bots** *to present "applause" prompts.*

Patterson   I am so pleased to acknowledge my dearest colleagues of the Council who—replete with wisdom and integrity, and graciousness and goodness— saw fit to pay tribute to the celebrated Citizen Jane by commissioning this Re-enacted Retrospective of her tireless service. Here at the Museum of Honors, here at the very edge of time itself, we are logged on. Logged in? At? . . . the Super Network, this wired-up for wireless grand magnificence of the modern age! Shaping our shared reality to the will of the dear clear Archival Architect-in-Residence—

He gives a grand gesture to **Jesse** *and continues the introduction.*

—whose artistic grasp of our great history is now reflected and refracted for your observation and appreciation!

Jesse   You mean my artistic grasp of our great history is now refracted and reflected for—

Patterson   The great history, abridged of course! Presented here for this marvelous occasion. Nothing less than the dramatic reenactment of the life and times of Citizen Jane, our super-shero. The Happy Endings We Deserve made manifest! Her Iconic Instances presented as homage, the glorious travails of the One and Only Heroine par Ex-cellence!

Enter **Citizen Jane** *in full persona and costume as superhero (including a glamorous wig and cape).*

She stands strong, basking in the light.

Jesse   Citizen Jane.

Patterson   Our champion, our defender, guardian, grand dame, mother, sister, lover, wife, daughter. Goddess. Our woman of wonder and light, Citizen Jane.

Excited like a schoolboy, **Jesse** *starts the* **Citizen Jane** *theme song:*

Jesse   She's amazing. She's terrific.

During the theme song, **Jane** *dances, giving the audience her signature superhero poses.*

Patterson   She's a wonder!

The **Bots** *are Jane's background dancers in perfect unison.*

Jesse   She's a marvel!

Citizen Jane *and the* **Bots** *do some great kicks and spins for the big finish.*

Patterson /Jesse   She's the best! The best! The best, the best, THE BEST!

Patterson *leads the applause and then gestures for* **Jesse** *to speak.*

Jesse   When I was approached by the Council to render her Greatest Moments, I had so much material to work with. The Happy Endings she has guaranteed are countless, how to choose?

Jane *and the* **Bots** *stand still as* **Jesse** *and* **Patterson** *continue their remarks.*

Patterson   Yes indeed. A conundrum to be sure. One could start at the "first beginning" I suppose—

Off "first beginning" **Patterson** *cues* **Jane** *and the* **Bots** *to reenact* **Jane**'s *origin story, as follows:*

Patterson   When the young and innocent girl Jane, ages and ages ago in the Utopian Realm of Many Waters, found her greatest destiny reflected in the Mirror of Marvels!

Dramatic reenactment: **Citizen Jane** *stands at the mirror, looking for herself.* (*The* **Bots** *assist.*)

Jesse   But the Citizen is timeless and who's to say which beginning is best? Some say her greatest moments, her truly Iconic Instances, were later. For example—

Patterson   Citizen Jane saves the darling baby child!

Jane *and the* **Bots** *drop the "Mirror Act" to re-enact the next scene:* **Citizen Jane** *saves the darling babe from a burning building.* (*The* **Bots** *assist on all reenactments.*)

Jesse   Yes! Or when Citizen Jane first battled the evil demon-monster-dragon hordes!

Jane *and company forget the baby for the next scene:* **Citizen Jane** *uses swords and guns to battle the evil demon-monster-dragon hordes.*

Patterson   With her bare hands.

Jane *and co. freeze and re-start the battle scene without weapons.*

Jesse   And Citizen Jane defeated the Criminally Cruel Mad Scientist, Dr. Devestato—

Patterson   —who tried to snatch Jane's DNA away to create a SUPER-EVIL CLONE of CITIZEN JANE!

Jesse   The EVIL CLONE—FEMME FATALIA—hated Citizen Jane to her core and soon joined forces with the sinister cyborg menace, ROBOTRIX, to terrorize all over!

Patterson   Yes. Yes! So Citizen Jane had to hustle and tussle and hunt them all down and deal with it! And she prevailed!

Dramatic reenactment of all the above. But **Citizen Jane** *is having a hard time keeping up.*

Citizen Jane   Patterson, I need transition time!

Patterson   Yes! Yes! Yes!

The theme song returns as **Jane** *catches up to the action.*

Jesse   She's amazing. She's terrific.

Citizen Jane *and the* **Bots** *rush to do the theme song dance/poses, but they are a few beats behind.*

Patterson/Jesse   She's a wonder! She's a marvel! She's the best! The best. The best, the best, THE BEST!

Patterson   You may now applaud, once more, in a manner befitting the occasion!

Audience applauds. **Jane** *pauses to take a break.*

Jesse   But Citizen Jane is always more than a warrior. Arch nemesis and terrorists aside, Citizen Jane is a super-shero for peace.

Off "peace" the **Bots** *drag* **Jane** *away before she can catch her breath to reenact as follows:*

Patterson   The Council couldn't agree with you more! Indeed, her peacemaking powers must be part of any retrospective. For starters, Citizen Jane is responsible for the first All-Around-the-World Peace Treaty. Signed by representatives of every grand nation, and even some negligibly important medium nations, even still some rather unremarkable non-important nations. Yes! All the countries signed the Treaty for World Peace for Ever and Ever!

After gathering signatures, **Citizen Jane** *brandishes her world peace treaty.*

Jesse   And then there was the All-Around-the Galaxy Peace Treaty, signed by the inner colonies, the outer colonies, the aliens, the robots, the other aliens, etcetera, etcetera.

Patterson   Etcetera, etcetera and so forth and so on! ALL SIGNED!

Citizen Jane *gathers even more signatures from all of the above in a frenzy.*

Citizen Jane (*worn out again*)   Good grief!

Jesse   But then, FEMME FATALIA returns, and Citizen Jane must battle battle battle the evil clone villainess!

Citizen Jane *discards her treaties and fights her clone some more.*

Patterson   And Femme Fatalia was working for CELESTE HALIBURPTON, the Corporate SuperEvil CEO, to guarantee the hungry children never got their new shoes for free! Citizen Jane beat the bitch down and liberated the charity goods for all the poor starving kiddies. And saved the economy!

Citizen Jane *uses her best moves to defeat her enemies.*

Patterson *applauds.* **Jesse** *applauds. The audience applauds.*

Patterson   And now, ever humble, our esteemed Citizen Jane will take her bow with graciousness and goodness.

Citizen Jane *takes her bow, but cuts it short. She flings off her cape and her wig in a dramatic flourish.*

Citizen Jane   Jesse. I'm tired.

Jesse   But Citizen Jane—

Jane   —can't go on like this. I didn't do these things.

Patterson   Who else but you, celebrated super-shero par ex-cellence, could do these wonders?

Jane   Reenacting the so-called Great History like this? Me. Me. Me. Every single time. These fantasies have run their course.

Patterson (*scandalized*)   Fantasies . . .?

Jesse   Jane—

Jane   I want this to stop, Jesse. I want this to stop now.

Patterson *gathers up* **Jane**'s *discarded trappings and tries to get* **Jane** *to go back to her super-shero self.*

Patterson   But . . . But when you were crowned Grand Benevolent Goddess Empress of the Universe and you stepped down to be among all the little people—

Jane *accepts her things from* **Patterson**, *eyeing* **Jesse** *all the while.*

Jane   There's no such thing as a Grand Benevolent Goddess Empress of the Universe, Patterson.

Patterson   Oh Citizen Jane . . . so modest.

As soon as **Patterson**'s *back is turned,* **Jane** *pushes the boots and such out of sight.*

Jesse   Citizen Jane—

Jane   Who am I, really?

She follows **Jesse**'s *gaze. He's looking at the control panels and the power cord at his feet.*

Jesse   You're the people's hero, Jane.

Jane   Is this really about the people?

Patterson   Here on the super-network, that's all that matters: providing for the people. You are the ultimate public servant, Citizen Jane. And we honor YOU for all the Happy Endings!

Jane   But who am I when I'm not saving the world, Jesse?

Jesse *has no answer.*

Jane I look for my reflection, in the mirror, in the water. I look and look . . . I don't see myself staring back, Jesse. Can you explain that to me?

Jesse We need you, Jane. Please.

Jane I look, keep hoping I'll find something real, something inside. But I can't. It's impossible for me. All I ever find is—

Jesse I never meant for it to go this far.

Jane —You.

Patterson Now this won't do. Not at all. Sowing discontent and confusion. Lies and deceit! Why, Citizen Jane would never make such declarations! No, there is only one possible conclusion: Villainy!

He clutches the podium in terror. **Jane** *is focused on* **Jesse**.

Jane Somehow I'm always . . . with you, and I prevail. I prevail. I prevail. Every enemy. Every challenge . . . I never lose. But this is the last time, Jesse. It has to be.

Jesse You are more than—

Patterson Impostor! This must be the EVIL FEMME FATALIA in the flesh! Help! I call upon the real Citizen Jane. Save us! Save us!

Jane's *attention is fixed on* **Jesse**.

Jane I'm some sort of alter-ego fantasy. Brought to life on your super-network. But not true.

Patterson No! No! No!

Jane I'm not my own self . . .

Patterson Audience members, you may now express displeasure befitting the occasion. Go on, boo. Boo the Evil Femme Fatalia Impostor!

He boos. The audience and **Bots** *join. It gets raucous.*

Jane Patterson, that's enough.

She uses her superpowers to freeze **Patterson** *in silence. The* **Bots** *get quiet.*

Jesse Without you, there's this shadow, Jane. Without you, when I open my eyes to actually see what's there . . .

A beat.

Jane I want my own happy ending, Jesse.

Jesse But you're nothing if not—

Jane —Then I'm nothing and you've lost nothing. Jesse, let me go. Let all of this go.

Jesse *considers and moves away from the podium.*

Jane *releases her power over* **Patterson**.

Patterson   But what about me? don't I have a say? I know I'm real.

Jane   Council member Ro Patterson—Third Generation—what do you find when you look for yourself? Who are you beyond this exhibition hall?

Patterson *looks to* **Jesse**.

Jesse   I'm sorry.

Jane   You have to move on, Jesse. Unplug.

Jesse *is breaking down.* **Patterson** *steps away from the podium, in true awe of* **Citizen Jane**.

Jesse   But if I do it, I'm not sure . . .

Jane   Neither am I . . . for the first time, I'm not sure.

Patterson   This was not in today's program, but may indeed be Citizen Jane at her finest.

Jane   Going forward. Living. leaving me be, leaving all this behind . . . Jesse can you do it?

A beat.

Jesse *reaches for the cord.*

He pulls the plug.

Patterson *vanishes. The* **Bots** *vanish.* **Jane** *finally vanishes.*

An unknown reality washes over **Jesse** *as the rest of the fantasy world disappears, leaving* **Jesse** *on the stage. Alone.*

End of Play.

Play #3: Vanna White Has Got to Die!
by Antoinette Nwandu

A young woman's insecurities about her future manifest in a "little voice inside her head" that is anything but helpful. Presented in The Fire This Time Festival Season 3, directed by Dan Rogers, performed by Felicia J. Hudson (**Seena**), Margaret Odette (**Vanna White**), and Stephen Heskett (**Charlie**).

Characters

Seena, *Black, young. A tender optimist and a bit of a loon. Seena speaks in a sugary falsetto.*
Charlie, *White, young. A doofus with a heart of gold. Seena's boyfriend.*
Vanna White, *a manifestation gone awry. A predator in whiteface. Pure rage.*

Time

Date night.

Place

Seena's kitchen.

Vanna White Has Got To Die! A Comedy *by Antoinette Nwandu*

A cramped apartment kitchen. Evening. **Seena** *enters the kitchen.*

Seena   No, really, it's fine. It's no trouble at all. I'll be back in a minute. Sit tight while I check on the pie.

Vanna White, *a manifestation, appears suddenly.*

Vanna   I cannot believe he just said that! Now dinner is ruined! And you went through all of this trouble!

Seena   Oh. Hello, Vanna White.

Vanna   Don't stand there and "oh hello" me. Who does he think he is?

Seena   He's Charlie, that's who.

Vanna   And that makes you what: just a girl with a sink full of dishes to clean?

Seena   Or the love of his life.

Vanna   Then how come he hasn't proposed?!

Seena   I don't know. But I'm hoping that maybe tonight after dinner—

Vanna   Just because you wear lipstick and bake him a pie . . .

Seena   Gotta go through his stomach to get to his heart.

Vanna *picks up a large knife. She and* **Seena** *tussle for it.*

Vanna   Not anymore, BabyCakes. He crossed the line. Now we're changing the plan.

Seena   Oh. We are?

Vanna   Eight-letter word. Starts with "H."

Seena   And the clue?

Vanna   It's the answer to all of our problems.

Seena   The word isn't HOMICIDE, is it?

Vanna   You guessed without picking a letter!

Seena   I'm checking the pie.

Vanna   It's not done.

Seena   How do you know?

Vanna   The plan is: We've got to kill Charlie!

Seena *grabs the knife from* **Vanna** *and hides it behind her back just as* **Charlie**, **Seena**'s *boyfriend, enters.*

Charlie   Hey, babe. You okay?

Seena   Just checking the pie!

Vanna   It's not done.

Charlie   Cuz, you know, that last comment—

Seena   What comment?! It's nothing! It's fine!

Vanna (*impersonating* **Charlie**)   Of course I'll be sure. Once I find the right person . . .

Charlie   I'm just nervous, that's all. Because I would never—Because, I have told you—Because, you and I—(*big sigh*) Seena, what can I do?

Vanna   You could finish a sentence!

Charlie (*to* **Vanna**)   I'm trying to talk to my girlfriend!

Vanna   *He* didn't say fiancée.

Charlie   I will when we get there.

Seena   I know.

Vanna   *If* we get there.

Charlie   You won't be invited!

Vanna   You threatening me, Chucky—boy?

Seena   Vanna White, that's enough!

Vanna   But he started—

Seena (*with the knife*)   I said that's enough! Charlie, go eat your mushroom risotto!

Charlie   You're kicking *me* out?

Vanna (*sing-songy*)   Sor-ry, Char-lie.

Seena   I need a few minutes.

Charlie   The voices you live with are very peculiar.

Seena   I know. But you love me regardless?

Charlie   I could use some more wine.

He exits with a bottle of wine.

Vanna   That didn't go very well.

Seena   No it didn't.

Vanna   Still think you're the love of his life?

Seena   I suppose.

Vanna   We should make him some coffee and lace it with bleach.

Seena   We're all out of the good stuff.

Vanna   Poke him to death with that brooch that he bought us.

Seena   And risk getting blood on the carpet?

Vanna   Turn up the gas and then light a cigar.

Seena   We're not killing Charlie!

Vanna   Why not? He deserves it.

Seena   I'm checking the pie.

Vanna   It's not done!

Seena   Then I'm going back out there.

Vanna   It's too late for that.

Seena   How do you know?

Vanna   Charlie wants to get rid of me, Seena. Because I'm so threatening.

Seena Silly goose. No he doesn't.

Vanna You know that I'm right.

Seena Charlie loves me and love means accepting the crazy. And you, silly goose, are the crazy.

Vanna I'm no mathematician, but I think your logic is faulty.

Seena He loves me I tell you!

Vanna But I love you more!

Seena Not a question of more. Not a question of choosing.

Vanna It will be to him. Mark my words.

Seena No it won't. Charlie knows you're my friend. He would never—

Vanna Oh, wouldn't he now . . .

Charlie *enters full of liquid courage.*

Charlie Alright, Seena. Enough is enough. You and I need to talk.

Vanna Here it comes.

Seena The risotto. It needs some more cheese.

Charlie It's about Vanna White. Three's a crowd and I want her to go.

Vanna It's so tough being right all the time.

Seena But I thought you accepted—

Charlie I did.

Seena It's this dinner. I shouldn't have pushed you—

Charlie No, Seena. It's bigger than that. I don't know if I can anymore.

Seena But you have to. I baked you a pie.

Charlie Either get rid of Vanna or lose me forever!

Seena YOU CAN'T MAKE ME LEAVE HER! SHE'S ALL THAT I'VE GOT!

Charlie Then what am I still doing here?

He turns to exit. **Vanna** *picks up the knife.*

Seena Wait, Charlie, please!

Charlie Yeah, Charlie. Wait just a minute.

Seena You said that you loved me.

Charlie I *do* love you, Seena.

Seena You said you could handle a little adventure.

Charlie   I thought that I could.

Vanna   So you lied?!

Charlie   I assumed she'd be out of the picture.

Vanna   You see that?! You see?! He's been planning to off me for months!

Charlie   What? No! Seena, I wouldn't. How could I?

Vanna   And sometimes when you're not around, I can tell that he's thinking of somebody else!

Seena   That blonde from your office.

Charlie   You're not really believing this, are you?

Seena   I wanted to marry you, Charlie.

Charlie   I wanted that too.

Vanna   Overrated!

Seena   And kids. And a house.

Vanna   Little brats and a mortgage you couldn't afford.

Seena   We had *je ne sais quoi*!

Charlie   We still do!

Seena   Then why are you leaving me, Charlie?

Charlie   Because Vanna White is insane! Plus, I'm still pretty sure that she doesn't exist.

Vanna   I don't exist? Honey, I've been her best friend ever since she was five. She would sit there for *hours* and watch as I walked back and forth turning white letter cubes in a bedazzled gown.

She hums a trance-like version of the Wheel of Fortune theme song while performing a letter-turning dance.

Seena (*entranced*)   So pretty. But what does it *mean*?

Vanna   Always be beaut-i-ful. Always be smile-ing.

Seena *joins in the hypnotic dance.*

Seena (*entranced*)   Always be beaut-i-ful. Always be smile-ing.

Vanna/Seena   Always be beaut-i-ful. Always be smile-ing.

Vanna   Just a matter of time til she let me get into that noggin of hers.

Charlie   This is crazy. You should have read books as a child!

Vanna   At least my show had letters!

Seena   I'm checking the pie!

Vanna   It's not done.

Charlie   You don't know that.

Vanna   How brown is the crust?

Seena   Pretty brown.

Vanna   Is it bubbling?

Seena   Not yet, I'm afraid.

Vanna   Then it needs some more time. Which is good because I have a plan.

Seena   Here we go.

Vanna (*big, with the knife*)   It's time to play WHEEL OF FORTUNE!

She takes **Charlie** *hostage.*

Charlie   Seena, listen to me. You can do this. You have to get rid of her!

Vanna   Ha! That's a laugh!

Charlie   Stay out of this! Seena can speak for herself!

Vanna   No she can't!

Charlie   Don't listen to her. Yes you can!

Vanna   Go ahead, Seena. Speak for yourself. Tell Chucky Boy here how that comment of his made you feel.

Seena   Really, Charlie. It's nothing. It's fine.

Vanna   See there? What did I tell you?

Charlie   Come on, Seena. Just tell me.

Seena   I can't, Charlie. Always be beaut-i-ful. Always be smile-ing.

Charlie   You don't mean that!

Seena   But what if you don't like what I have to say?

Vanna   He'll desert you forever. You'll cry, then you'll go buy a cat!

Charlie   I'll listen to you, like you listen to me.

Seena   What if we never agree and we turn into miserable people?

Charlie   We'll figure it out step-by-step.

Seena   It's too scary. I don't think I can.

Charlie   But she's going to kill me!

Seena   Vanna, no! You can't do this! I don't want to lose him!

Vanna   Get out of my way, little girl, before I kill you *both*!

Charlie   Wait a minute! If Vanna White lives in your mind, then your mind needs to go somewhere she's never been.

Vanna   Like she'd ever go someplace without me. Admit it. I'm everything to her.

Charlie   How about that time by the lake?

Seena   She was there.

Vanna   Yes, I was and your game was pathetic.

Charlie   That time we had lunch with my mother?

Vanna   Please tell me you're kidding.

Charlie   This is crazy. There must be some moment where you have been something!

Seena   Wait a minute, there was that one time! On our first hipster date!

Charlie   We did laundry together!

Vanna   Puh-leeze. I was there.

Seena   I don't think so. You hate doing chores.

Charlie   Quick, Seena. Jump to that memory!

Vanna   When did you learn how to TELEPORT?!

Charlie and **Seena** *teleport to the laundromat. Early in the relationship. Awkward-cute.*

Vanna *watches from the present.*

Charlie   Hey, babe. What's the matter?

Seena   It's nothing.

Charlie   No, Seena. We came to change history. Now, tell me the truth!

Seena   It's too hard.

Charlie   But it's our only hope!

Seena   You put your red shirt in my whites. Now my socks are all pink.

Charlie   Whatever, it's not a big deal.

Seena   It's . . . a . . . big . . . deal to me!

Suddenly, **Vanna** *jerks uncontrollably.*

Seena   Look, Charlie. It's working! I told you the truth and then Vanna got weaker!

Vanna   Always be beaut-i-ful! Always be smile-ing!

Charlie   Quick, Seena! Back to the present and say something else!

Seena and **Charlie** *teleport back to the present.*

Seena   That comment you made hurt my feelings!

More **Vanna** *wiggles and zaps.*

Charlie   I know. It was stupid. I'm sorry.

Seena   Most of the time, I order takeout!

More **Vanna** *wiggles and zaps.*

Charlie   Number six with a side of black beans, hold the peppers.

Seena (*fake/real voice*)   This isn't / my actual voice.

Vanna *wiggles and zaps to her doom.*

Charlie   This whole time?

Seena   I was trying to be Vanna White for you, Charlie.

Charlie   But *you* are the woman I love. The real you.

Seena   I love you!

Vanna   Wait! Wait! Please! Don't kill me!

Charlie   Why not?

DING! The oven.

Vanna   Cuz . . . it's . . . time . . . to . . . serve . . . pie!

She reaches desperately for the pie. And then dies!

Charlie   Quick, Seena. Grab it!

Seena (*triumphantly holding the pie*)   I did it. I killed Vanna White.

Charlie (*down on one knee, with a ring*)   What a relief. Will you marry me, Seena?

Seena   Of course I will, Charlie. Now let's go eat some pie.

Charlie   After you . . .

Play #4: Hard Palate *by Roger Q. Mason*

In the age of dating apps and PrEP, Quentin battles old stigmas about gay sex that thwart Clayton's courtship of him. Presented in The Fire This Time Festival Season 7, directed by Nicole A. Watson, performed by Pierre Jean Gonzalez (**Quentin**), Kareem M. Lucas (**Clayton**), and Erika Grob (**Brooke Shields**).

Character Breakdown

Quentin, *twenties, Black male—his mother's Catholic background fuels his inner shame; a writer by trade; a worrier by preoccupation; little concerns grow to catatonic anxieties, affecting him in love and maybe fiercely articulate, though he plays aloof for "the men" because he thinks that's what they want; he's not of the ideal size either—he's soft, a little thick, and not too athletic.*
Clayton, *twenties, African American—he is a rapper by trade, but works one of those "American dream jobs" to pay the bills: you know the type, like Walmart or the local drugstore, or Chuck E. Cheese, those places with incentives which give a centimeter but make it feel like you've gone ten miles; he's dedicated to his work, particularly now that it's what keeps him going; he is HIV positive, but he doesn't want it to define him; he wants to be seen as a gentleman and a lover, let the meds and discretion take care of the rest.*
Brooke Shields, *forties, white female—she doesn't need to look a thing like the real Ms. Shields, but that essence of authority and trustworthiness are essential; she can sell you anything, especially your wildest nightmare.*

Hard Palate: A Short Play *by Roger Q. Mason*

*In darkness, a cell phone rings. It grows louder and louder. We fade in on **Quentin**, frozen in ecstasy watching his phone ring. A man has called him from his favorite sex app. Success! Then, the moment is squelched by . . . a reliable white woman who appears on screen, as if right over his right shoulder—Jiminy Cricket style. Oh lawd!*

Brooke Shields   Don't answer it.

Quentin *freezes her with a gesture. He turns to speak to us through the camera.*

Quentin   This is my fear.

*She pushes past the freeze, as if her will to express herself and police **Quentin** are too much for his black boi metatheater magic. (The following dialogue should roll like almost overlapping banter. I'll indicate the beginning and end of the sequence with ***.)*

*****Brooke**   Don't answer that call.

Quentin (*to her*)   I already did.

Brooke   Why'd you give him your number?

Quentin   She can sell you anything.

Brooke   These phones are like trackers.

Quentin   Like eyelash lengthener.

Brooke   He knows where we are!

Quentin   A Lazy Boy.

Brooke   He can find you. Day or night.

Quentin   B-grade eye glasses.

Brooke   Now you have nothing to protect you from him. Whatever thin veil of anonymity you once had has been tragically thrown away!

Quentin   Or the feeling of terminal illness when you sit next to that guy scratching his scabbed arm on the bus. But I've got her under control now.

***Her rant may continue for a bit with some ad lib. Here's suggested language below . . .*

Brooke   What if he's a converted divorcee, a stalker, a basher . . .

Quentin   Hey!

Brooke   A slasher, a thrasher,

Quentin   Uh uh, gurl. Not on today.

Brooke   A giver of thrash.

Quentin   Miss Brooke.

Brooke   My God. Your poor throat itching, pulsing, rasping . . . you're done for good.

Quentin   MISS BROOKE!

She stops immediately.

Quentin   No, ma'am. Get yo'self together. Breathe in self-assurance.

Brooke   Self-assurance.

Quentin   Breathe out fret.

Brooke   Out . . . fret . . .

Quentin   Again.

He looks **Brooke** *dead in the eye. They breathe together.*

Quentin   We good?

Brooke *exhales and nods her head in meek agreement*

Quentin (*to* **Brooke**)   Good. Let's try this one mo' time. (*To his phone.*) Hey, man. Can you hear me now? I'm soooo sorry. I think my phone's fucked. Bad reception or some shit. I'm at the end of my contract and I swear these things are set to self-destruct. Can you hear me now?

Clayton   Yeah, man. No worries. I feel you.

Quentin *melts at the sound of his voice.*

Quentin (*to the audience*)   Oh. My. God! Do . . . you . . . hear . . . that . . . VOICE?! He's masc. Mmmmmmmm. So. Masc. Like so so so . . .

Clayton   Huh?

Quentin   Shit.

Clayton   You say something?

Quentin (*cleaning up and clearing his throat*)   You . . . were saying your name.

Clayton   Right. I'm Clayton.

Quentin   Hey, Clay. (*Pause.*) Can I call you that? I really hope it's okay. I'm just jumping off a ledge here. Cuz, to be fair, you are just "C" on the app, Clay, Clayton, sorry, and . . . are you trying to telegraph some sort of gender neutrality through that gesture of naming? I mean, that's cool if you are. I'm here for it. I am mos def your ally in that choice and I will defend it before any one of these fuckers who thinks they can . . . I'm assuming. Oh God. Now you're offended. You're quiet because I've offended you.

I've overstepped and overstayed my welcome in your ear space and . . . Hello? Are you still there? If you're not, I completely understand. This is all on me. Hello? Oh fuck.

Clayton   You're cute.

Quentin   . . . Really?

Clayton   I mean, you think too much, but . . .

Quentin   I should just crawl under my little rock now and die.

Clayton   No need for a big drama, man. Just an observation. It's cool. I mean, I think too much too sometimes. But shit, you got a lot going on up there.

Quentin   You have no idea.

Quentin *looks at* **Brooke**. *She's been listening the whole time, but now she's in view; she's finds herself in lotus pose meditating, one eye closed, the other open but unseen by* **Quentin**.

Clayton   You gotta relax sometimes, fam. Shut it down. Hey, what're you doing tonight?

Quentin *looks to* **Brooke** *for guidance, who belligerently meditates. She breaks out of it for a moment.*

Brooke   So soon? Mmmmm.

Then goes back to meditation. **Quentin** *is on his own for this one. He makes a decision about the course of the conversation for himself—without* **Brooke**'s *help or consent.*

Quentin   What did you have in mind?

Clayton   I'm at twenty-four.

Quentin   Where?

Clayton   24-Hour Fitness. The gym. You go?

Quentin (*lying*)   Oh yeah! All the time.

While **Quentin** *looks at his abdomen, soft and a little bit round,* **Brooke** *has crept slowly to peer over* **Quentin**'s *shoulder. She grabs his phone, and he's taken aback.*

Hey, give it back!

Brooke   He's a rapper.

Quentin   Quit looking at that.

Brooke   His hat is on backwards.

Quentin   Hand me my phone.

Brooke   He wears hoodies and too-big t-shirts. Is this what you like?

Quentin   He's nice. He texted me voluntarily—unprompted. I didn't have to do a thing. That's never happened before.

Brooke   He's a predator. You're his dead meat for the night.

Quentin   Just give me my fucking—

Brooke   Maybe he's on the DL.

She starts texting **Clayton** *on the phone.*

Sorry, my brotha, I don't think this is gonna pan out, you dig?

Quentin   What the hell is your problem? I don't sound like that. This isn't 1967.

Brooke   I'm just trying to help you. Keep you safe and out of trouble.

A beat. **Quentin** *regards what* **Brooke** *says, then shakes it off.*

Quentin   Trouble isn't lurking around the corner. Trouble's not lurking around the corner. Trouble is not lurking around the corner.

Clayton   You alright, man? Seems like there's some kinda drama going on over there.

Quentin   We're all good over here.

Clayton   Who's we? If you're with your people, I can . . .

Brooke   You want to go to that gym, don't you. Do it. But, just remember . . . it's dangerous out there.

Quentin   Hey, Clay . . .

Should he go to the gym or should he not? He decides.

My phone's about to die. I think I should . . .

He closes his phone. Lights change. The phone rings again. **Clayton** *appears.*

Brooke *is chanting "om shanti shanti shanti" while pacing around and* **Quentin** *is studying his phone, contemplating his next move.*

Quentin   He asked me where I lived. What should I tell him?

Brooke   Whatever you want.

Quentin   Excuse me?

Brooke   You heard me. Tell him whatever you want.

Quentin   What's gotten into you? You're so . . .

Brooke   You're grown. You know what's best for you.

Clayton   . . . that's what I thought. The app was saying you were like .2 miles away, whatever that ish means.

Quentin   Yeah, I live two blocks away from the gym.

Brooke   Ask him to come over.

Quentin (*to* **Brooke**)   What? (*to* **Clay**)

Brooke   Let him come over . . .

Quentin   Are you there right now?

Clayton   Yeah. I'm by the gym right now.

Brooke   Tell him to come over so your mother can see.

Quentin   She won't know. I have him come to the back of the house.

Brooke   There you go sneaking. That's where it starts.

Quentin   I'm an adult. I may still live at home, but I'm old enough. I can do what I want. Hell, he'll come through the front door.

Brooke   When he comes through the front, will you be ready?

Quentin   Sure.

Brooke   For the screaming and the crying and the pangs of the ages? The "What did I do to deserve this, I am a good mother?" The ten "Hail Marys" and no red meat for a month to cleanse her soul. You'll break her. Hasn't the poor woman been through enough?

Quentin   She'll have to get over it. This is who I am. (*To* **Clayton**.) You're still at the gym? I can come over if you like.

Clayton   Yeah, I'm still here. In the sauna.

Quentin   The sauna, how sweaty.

Clayton   How often do you really come to this gym?

Quentin   Um, all the time. I was there last night.

Clayon   There's no sauna.

Quentin   Oh.

Clayton   It's cool. We all got secrets. (*Beat.*) You don't need it, papi. The gym, I mean.

Quentin   Ha! Yes I do. My thighs make thunder, my chest is an emerging B cup, my sides are . . .

Clayton   You don't need it. You look fine.

Quentin   You've seen my pictures?

Clayon   Yeah, man.

Quentin   All of them? Even those from the gourmet phase of last spring?

Clayton   Haha, yeah, dude. I like what I see.

Silence.

Let's hang out sometime. Like, for real and shit. Not on this phone. Would you like that?

Quentin   Yeah, I would.

Clayton   Cool. Text me when you're free . . . baby.

The phone hangs up. **Quentin** *holds it in his hand under its spell.*

Quentin (*to the audience*)   Did you see that? He asked me out. He asked me out! Me. Not that thin little white boy who cuts his hair short, squints his eyes, dirties his nails, and quotes Foucault and Tupac to attract a cosmopolitan "brotha"; not one of these hard, muscled chocolate love dreams who went vegan for religious reasons then stayed cuz it made him look good; not the next half-European, half-Asian, half-whatever pan-human whose green eyes and pink lips haunt every postmodern wet dream. No. Me. Stalky brown me. He likes me, I can feel it.

Brooke   You don't know about him.

Quentin   I thought you were in lotus pose meditating on leaving my ass alone.

Brooke   I was, till you stopped using common sense. What's his name?

Quentin   Clayton.

Brooke   His last name?

Quentin   I don't know.

Brooke   You should.

Quentin   It's not important. That kinda stuff doesn't matter. People don't give things like that out anymore. And if you ask for them, you look like a stalker.

Brooke   You would trust this man?

Quentin   He's really nice.

Brooke   You met him on a hook-up app.

Quentin   He's different.

Brooke   You don't know that. Who he's been with? Where his mouth's been?

Quentin   He asked me out on a date.

Brooke   Why would he ask *you* out?

Quentin   Because . . .

Brooke   These little indiscretions—

Quentin   You disgust me.

Brooke   What do you want him to do to you?

Quentin   I want what every human wants.

Brooke   That's where it all starts. Little slips in judgments.

Quentin   I'm a virgin because of you. The things you put in my head. I've got carpel tunnel from all the jacking off I do. I want the real thing. I deserve it. I want Clayton.

Brooke   A few compliments and you're head over heels, just like a desperate little hussy.

Quentin   Fuck you! Leave me alone. Get off of my back. I am going to live my life. I am too old for your shit. Go! I don't need you around me anymore.

Brooke   Good look, Quentin Brickstone. You'll need it.

She storms off.

Quentin (*to the audience*)   I have spent my entire life listening to her. She's full of shit. Do you know I had a phase during the first avian flu epidemic where I washed my hands every time I touched a door because I was sure I'd get it. My knuckles cracked and bled for a month. For years I have made sure to put down at least twelve toilet safety guards when I sit down in a public rest room. Any more and the pipes overflow (*that's happened*). Any less and something will seep through, I'm sure of it—someone's herpes lurking or the clap hopping for a new host, or—Fuck this!

Clayton is nice. He thinks I'm cute. He's pursuing me. I don't even have to try. And it feels good. He's fine. He goes to the gym. He's healthy. He does chest and back and cardio. He's fine. Right. Right?

Lights change. **Clayton** *and* **Quentin** *stand in front of each other.* **Clayton** *has flowers behind his back.* **Quentin** *is beaming.*

Clayton   Happy birthday.

Quentin   Really?

Clayton   It's not?

Quentin   No, no. It is! You're so sweet.

Clayton *kisses* **Quentin**. **Quentin** *is stunned, silence and sprung. He tastes someone else's DNA sliding warmly down his throat.*

Clayton   We skipped a step. My bad. I mean, the first date is supposed to be coffee or whatever, but we already kicking it and now there's a kiss involved, so now we're in a situation.

Quentin   You don't see me complaining . . . baby. Why're you so nice, Clayton?

Clayton   Shouldn't I be? That's the problem now. No gentlemen left in the world. Are the burgers here good?

Quentin   Hell yeah. Sometimes I order two.

Clayton   Thank God you can eat.

Quentin   Excuse me?

Clayton   You keep it real. Some of these fools order a side salad and eat half. That's some bullshit, cuz. I know you hungry. Where's the head? I should wash up.

Quentin   You want me to show you?

Clayton   Maybe . . .

Lights change.

Quentin   We started something in the bathroom.

Clayton   Chill, Q. We're in the street, man.

Quentin   I'd like to finish it.

Clayton   Slow down, b.

Quentin   It's my birthday. Your lips are so sweet. I'd like to taste them all night.

Quentin *reaches into* **Clayton**'s *pants.*

Clayton   You don't know me like that yet.

Quentin   This is my night. I feel safe with you. Come here.

He fellates **Clayton**.

Clayton   Q, I'm positive.

Quentin   Me too. I want you. People can watch. The danger makes me hot.

Clayton   I have HIV . . . but you can't get it from kissing.

A thousand shards of broken glass fall from the sky. **Quentin** *is mortified.*

Quentin   I did more than kiss you.

Brook *enters wearing red—shuddering, standing between* **Quentin** *on one side of the stage and* **Clayton** *on the other. The three of them speak in a round.*

Brooke   Your mouth. His head.

Quentin   There's a scratch. On the roof of my mouth. My hard palate. It was the fries, I'm sure.

Brooke   Those little indiscretions.

Clayton   I've got it under control. My cocktail is good. My viral loads are low.

Brooke   His dick dripping cum, no precum, whatever.

Clayton   It felt so good to be warm again. For someone to see *me*, not my . . .

Brooke   Danger seeping into you. The things we fear coming true.

Quentin   I've got it now.

Clayton   No you don't, man. Everything's cool.

Quentin   I'm done for. I might as well be dead.

Clayton   Now all you see is my disease.

Brooke   Oh God.

Quentin   OH MY GOD! Oh my God!

Quentin *and* **Brooke** *start to clench their chests. They are both having trouble breathing.* **Brooke** *draws closer and closer to* **Quentin***, trying to reach for his neck.* **Clayton** *sees* **Quentin** *gasping.*

Clayton   Q! Quentin. Baby! Please just . . .

He starts running towards **Quentin***, who doesn't notice him because but he's in a holy battle with* **Brooke**. **Quentin** *wrestles* **Brooke***'s hands from his neck and pushes her to the ground.* **Clayton** *can't see* **Brooke***, but he hears everything* **Quentin** *says, and he's taken aback.*

Quentin (*to* **Brooke**)   Stop! Stop breathing so hard because there's nothing to worry about any longer. He's given it to me. Okay? The gift. And it's only going to be a matter of time before it festers and fills me up. And you know what, I feel relieved. Because now I don't have to sit on pins and needles worrying about who I suck off and who puts his dick in my ass. I am free. And there's nothing you can do to stop me now because it doesn't matter, and I don't give a fuck. So go. Get lost. Find somebody else to save, cuz I'm fucked up already and there's no use wasting your time on me.

Brooke *sits on the ground, shivering, catatonic. She's at a loss for words.* **Quentin** *stares triumphantly over her.* **Clayton**'*s voice breaks him from this quiet revelry.*

Clayton   You're sick, man. It doesn't work that way. Happy birthday, again.

He walks away.

Quentin   No. Wait. Please. I know that's not how it works. Believe me. That's just what I needed to tell her—

Clayton   Her?

Quentin   Um . . . (*Pause.*) see . . . (*Pause.*) she's . . .—

Clayton   Who's she, man? Who are you talking to?

Quentin *looks back at where* **Brooke** *was. She's gone, not there.*

Quentin   No one. It's just me. Me and . . . you.

Clayton   Yeah, me and you.

Quentin   I like this.

Clayton   I do too.

He starts walking away. **Quentin** *grabs him by the waist.* **Clayton** *freezes in wistful anticipation. Out of the corner of his eye,* **Quentin** *sees* **Brooke** *has been making a long, slow, painful exit upstage.* **Quentin** *buries his head in* **Clayton**'*s chest. He hears his breath pattern and begins breathing in the same rhythm. They inhale and exhale as one.* **Clayton** *and* **Quentin** *grow unified in breath—calm, together, complete, their breaths entering and exiting through their hard palates. The two men inhale and exhale one long full breath together. It is a sigh of relief. They are one.*

Lights out.

Section 2

The Cost of Education: Confronting the Effects of Racial Disparity in America's Education System

Education in America has long been held up as the gateway to social mobility. For Black Americans some of the biggest fights for equality are still waged in the classroom. While the Civil Rights Act of 1964 granted Black children the right to attend schools with white children, disparity in education along racial lines persisted due to the systemic racism that deprives Black families and neighborhoods of the resources that their white neighbors have. Over the past decade in America, the wealth and racial gap has only widened, further deepening the differences in access to resources and opportunities in education. Dominique Morisseau's play *Third Grade* shows the effects of an underfunded, unfair system on not only the educators and students in Black communities, but the parents as well. Tracey Conyer Lee's play *Poor Posturing* examines how the racial disparities in education at the lower level can morph into a more insidious inequality at the higher levels of education. And Francisca Da Silveira's play *scholarship babies* dramatizes the often difficult leap for students of color from grade school education into the world of elite universities.

Foreword by Cynthia G. Robinson, The Fire This Time Season 4 playwright, The Fire This Time's New Works Lab leader, and longtime educator

My two professional passions are playwriting and teaching. Teaching has afforded me a deep well of stories to tell, and theater has afforded me the platform on which to tell them ... I began my teaching career at an elite private school on the upper westside of Manhattan. I was hired to teach English, grades 6 through 8. Working there set the foundation for my career in education, which at the time of this writing spans 29 years. "The Upper School" was a private institution, funded by hefty tuition and endowments; a space of privilege, designed for student success. No school is perfect, but this was a place that had intentionally built a foundation that served students and encouraged teaching and learning in and out of the classroom. From an educational standpoint, it was a bucolic place to teach; however, it was lacking in racial and cultural diversity among the student body, faculty, and administration. During my tenure at "The Upper School," I was gifted one of the most profound and personally gratifying relationships of my life. I met a twelve-year-old girl named Shelley. She was one of the handful of Black children at the school, and I was the only Black teacher there (in a faculty of twenty teachers). We were meant to be together. She followed me everywhere and was always at my desk in the common room. We were each other's missing link in this white space. I became close with her family and acted as her advocate during faculty meetings where micro-and macro-aggressions towards Black children were prevalent. As a young Black woman, I was called to speak up against systemic racism on the ground level. This was both empowering and exhausting.

Education in America is an enormous and complicated issue, heavily interwoven with the issues of race and economics. I believe the obstacle, however, is by no means insurmountable and teachers are at the front lines of narrowing the gap in their remote and in-person classrooms.

Play #5: Third Grade *by Dominique Morisseau*

An overworked teacher and a concerned parent try to find common ground at the end of a very long day.

Presented in The Fire This Time Festival Season 2, directed by Monica L. Williams, performed by Andrea Patterson (**Kai**) and Louis Martinez (**Steele**).

Characters

Kai, *Black or Latina woman. Early thirties. Teacher. Dedicated. Concerned.*
Steele, *Black or Latino man. Late twenties/early thirties. Father. Streetwise. Serious. Uncompromising.*

Setting

A New York City public school classroom. Present.

Note about Play

Race is important in this play in a very subtle way. In particular, please pay close attention to casting. Everyone should feel like they are a vested part of inner-city New York. Anything that throws off this balance or raises different dynamics is wrong. This is not a "great white hope" play. It's an interior dilemma that will hopefully inspire universal solutions.

Thank you for understanding this!

Third Grade: A Ten-Minute Play *by Dominique Morisseau*

A pool of light up on **Kai**. *She sits on her teacher's desk.*

Kai   Another late night at work. Revamping the lesson plans yet again. I still can't figure out how to make my students comprehend. Today's class was painful. Sharee is not understanding the difference between nouns and pronouns and when I try to help her, she starts crying profusely. I think she's afraid of being wrong. Maya keeps falling asleep on the math lessons. Her family doesn't make her go to bed at night so . . . Malcolm and Leland have become the new class bullies no matter how many times I separate them. I tried calling their parents, and the father accused me of picking on them. And no matter how many times I asked Jason to remove his hat, he refused. The third-grade practice test is coming up, and I am very concerned for my students. I want to be effective. Get them to the next level. If they fail . . . then so do I . . . and for this, I am frightened . . .

Lights up full on a classroom. **Kai** *shuffles through papers. A young father,* **Steele,** *enters the room.*

Steele   You Ms. Mattison?

Kai   The kids call me Ms. M. But please, call me Kai.

Steele   You my son's teacher?

Kai   Well . . . let's see . . . who's your son?

Steele   Jason. Jason Steele.

Kai   Oh yes – Jason. Yes, I'm his teacher. I've never met you before. You're Mr. Steele?

Steele   Yeah.

Kai   Well, Mr. Steele, it's quite late. The school is actually closed right now. But I can talk for a moment about Jason, if you like. Did Eddie let you in?

Steele   Yeah. He tol' me what you did.

Kai   What I did?

Steele   How you was disrespectin' him.

Kai   Eddie?

Steele   Naw. My son.

Kai   Mr. Steele, I don't disrespect my students. Whatever Jason told you, he's exaggerating.

Steele   You ask him to take off his hat?

Kai   I did. But that's hardly disrespect. It's school policy. Students take off their hats. I just enforce the rules.

Steele   Why you gotta embarrass my son for?

Kai   It's not about embarrassment. If Jason's not listening, I'm going to target him so that he understands his defiance is not acceptable.

Steele   You seen his hair?

Kai   I haven't. He refused to take off his hat today. I gave up fighting.

Steele   You seen his hair?

Kai   No, Mr. Steele, I haven't seen his hair.

Steele   It's burnt.

Kai   What?

Steele   He burnt it. Hair caught on fire.

Kai   I had no idea Jason was in a fire. The school didn't report—

Steele   Wasn't no house fire. He was just playin' around with matches. Him and his brother. I told their mama not to leave her matches around, but she smoke too much and can't nobody make her quit. So they found 'em and started playin' with 'em. His brother lit his hair on fire. I had to pat it out.

Kai   I had no idea.

Steele   His hair is burnt. It's uneven. Don't nothin' make it look right. Not even when his mama cornrow it. It look crazy—you know what I'm sayin'?

Kai   I think I understand. Perhaps you could write him a note, Mr. Steele . . . he could bring it to class, and then I could allow him to keep his hat on—

Steele   It's too late. You already messed up.

Kai   Messed up? What are you.

Steele   I didn't come here to talk this out. I came here to settle some shit.

Kai   Mr. Steele, I'm not sure I understand . . . but if you came to cause some kind of trouble.

Steele   You know what they did to him?

Kai   Who?

Steele   Them kids. Them boys that's in yo' class. The ones always be messin' with J.

Kai   If you're talking about Leland and Malcolm, don't worry. I've called their parents today. They've been bothering everyone.

Steele   You know what they did?

Kai   No . . . I don't . . . I don't know what they did.

Steele   They chased him—after school. Chased him to the dead end. That's where they cut him.

Kai   What?

Steele   You know yo' kids got blades?

Kai   They . . . they're third graders . . . I—

Steele   You know?

Kai   No. I didn't know.

Steele   Jason's at the hospital.

Kai   Is he alright?!

Steele   He's with his mama. Gonna pull through. Coulda been fatal.

Kai   Oh my God . . . is there something I can do?

Steele   You shouldna messed with him, lady.

Kai   I didn't . . . (*Sigh.*) . . . Mr. Steele, I'm trying to explain—

Steele   Jason's a good kid.

Kai   I know he is. And he's very bright too.

Steele   He wanted to learn.

Kai   He's still learning.

Steele   I'm his father.

Kai   I understand.

Steele   He's my only son—know what I'm sayin'? I gotta protect.

Kai   Mr. Steele, I understand how you feel . . . but I'm not Jason's enemy.

Steele   It's like the knifin' . . . that happens. Kids gotta 'fend for theyselves sometimes. But the embarrassment . . . you know what I'm sayin'? That's like the shit that stays with you. You embarrassed him.

Kai   I just asked him to take off his hat.

Steele   All day you asked him—til it got them boys curious 'bout why he wouldn't take it off. You made my son a target. You made him weak.

Kai   Mr. Steele, Jason isn't weak. He's young.

Steele   You hear me? You made him look soft. Them boys thought they could run him.

Kai   I can't believe—

Steele   Believe.

Kai   Mr. Steele, I know you're upset. You have every right to be. But I'm not Jason's enemy. If you give me a chance to think . . . maybe I can call Leland and Malcolm's parents again—

Steele   What's callin' his parents s'pose to do?

Kai   We can put our heads together and figure out how to take action—

Steele   I'm takin' action.

Kai   What do you mean?

Steele   I want addresses. To these kids' houses. I want 'em now.

Kai   I can't . . . I won't. . . . I don't want you to do something dangerous. Jason needs you—

Steele   Jason's got me. I'm his father—understand?

Kai   I know you're his father.

Steele   Then find those addresses.

Kai   What do you plan to . . . . what do you think you're going to . . . do?

Steele   Askin' stupid questions? I'm gonna handle this. Let Jason get his honor back. That's what.

Kai   By what—fighting? Hurting these kids? Their families? That's not going to solve anything—

Steele   It'll solve it for now. No solution is permanent. Everything temporary til the next battle.

Kai   We had parent–teacher conferences two weeks ago.

Steele   So?

Kai   I didn't see you there.

Steele   You bein' smart?

Kai   I'm being direct. The third grade regents are approaching. Jason needs to pass or he'll stay behind. You want to give him honor? Help him study.

Steele   Naa. You ain't failin' Jason.

Kai   Won't be my choice. It'll be the State's.

Steele   You his teacher. Figure it out.

Kai   It's not just . . . it can't just be me. He needs more. You.

Steele   He's got me.

Kai   It would've been nice—to meet you, is all I'm saying. At the conferences.

Steele   Where you been?

Kai   Excuse me?

Steele   His second-grade teacher, Miss Porter? Used to bring him home sometimes after school. Make sure he got home safe if he was in trouble.

Kai   You're saying I should bring him home? That's not my job, Mr. Steele. I'm not Miss Porter. I have a lot of other—

Steele   Can't be just you right?

Kai   That's right.

Steele   Can't be just me either.

Kai   He's your . . . son . . .

Steele   You think I don't take good care of my son?

Kai   I didn't say that.

Steele   I teach him what I know.

Kai   Well, that's good but.

Steele   Survival. That's what I know. Never a sign of weakness. Inferiority. Vulnerability. It will make you disappear out here. You understand? These streets will vaporize you. That's what I know. That's my care. Survive.

Kai   And if he survives all of this and can't read or do math? He'll still be inferior.

Steele   You got those addresses?

Kai   I won't. I am not giving you the addresses, Mr. Steele. That is not how we do things here. It's against school policy.

Steele (*moving toward* **Kai** *threateningly*)   I look like I give a shit about school policy?

Kai   Will you . . . hurt me too? Threaten me for this?

Steele   This is what I can do. For my son. I'm his father, you understand? I'm here. Present. Available. His defender. If he doesn't have me, who's he got?

Kai   He needs you. But not like this.

Steele   Not like this? (*Beat.*) Why you teach here?

Kai   Excuse me?

Steele   This hood. This school. You chose it?

Kai   I . . . what does that. . . .

Steele   Or was you sent here. Default. Not your first pick.

Kai   What does that matter, Mr. Steele? I'm here. I'm at this school. I'm committed. I stay late to get my students prepared and ready for the next day. What difference does it make if this school was or was not my first choice? I'm here!

Steele   It makes a difference. You here by default. Just like us. Default. Didn't choose this school. Didn't choose this block. Didn't choose this life. It chose us. Got dealt to us. Just like you. Fucked-up hand that you gotta play out. Make due. And we play the games we good at, Ms. Mattison. The games we master. Stay away from the ones we never learned how to play, cuz nobody has time to lose for the sake of playin' around. Don't have time to try and fail cuz failure is death. It's the end. So you do what you gotta do now. You play what you know. This is what I know. And I want those addresses that you keep in that desk of yours with all kinds of afterschool papers and homework and toys you took from kids and pencils and whatever the fuck. The forms you use to call home to parents and complain to us about how our kids aren't behaving and your limited classroom management skills don't know how to put a kid in a corner or send him outta the fuckin' room rather than ruining my time that could be better spent makin' this paper so I can afford to keep a meal in my kid's mouth. It's default. All of us here by default. And I'm playin' what I know so I can win. Cuz if I lose . . . I lose way too much. You get me?

Kai   I get you.

She goes to the desk. Pulls out some forms. Hands them to **Steele**.

Kai   These are the after-school forms for Leland and Malcolm. Leland's parents—the Gomez family. The mother is in the hospital. The father works double shifts for Sanitation. Malcolm lives with his grandmother. She's just recovering from kidney stone removal. Here, Mr. Steele. Go play your game. Go win back Jason's honor at all costs. Even at his own cost. Make him hard. Make him as steel as his last name. But he's eight years old. I'm sorry he got cut. I'm sorry Malcolm and Leland are so angry and frustrated that they don't know what to do. But they're little boys. Third graders. And they just need to be reminded of that. Give them a toy . . . compliment their work . . . give them a gold star . . . and you'll see them change before your eyes. Their faces instantly youthful. They are children. And how they survive is by being that— children. Keeping their youth. Not having it toughened out of them. (*Beat.*) Here, Mr. Steele. Take them. Go. Win for Jason. If you can . . .

Steele *looks at* **Kai**. *Long moment. Finally, he takes the forms and heads to the door.*

Steele   I'm a good father. I got my son's back. That's more than most people got. (*Beat.*) He's gonna win.

He toils with the forms . . . and disappears behind the door.

Kai *exhales. Sits at her desk in exhaustion.*

A pool of light encircles her.

Kai   Every night at work . . . more challenging than the one before. I am holding my breath for my students every day. Holding my breath when they take a test. Holding my breath when I ask for homework. Holding my breath when they go to lunch and return and hopefully haven't gotten in a fight. Holding my breath when they go home. Hoping they'll be fed. Be nourished. Be helped. Be bathed and put to bed. Holding my breath the entire semester while I prepare them for . . . the next level. Hoping that they make it. Hoping that they pass. Holding my breath until . . . they win . . .

Blackout.

Play #6: Poor Posturing *by Tracey Conyer Lee*

A professor tries to rationalize away the likelihood that she's treating one of her African American students unfairly. Presented in The Fire This Time Festival Season 4, directed by Kevin R. Free, performed by Sara Thigpen (**Rachel**), Chinaza Uche (**Demetrius**), and Lisa Rosetta Strum (**Cecily**).

Characters

Rachel, *a white college professor.*
Demetrius, *a Black college student.*
Cecily, *a Black college professor, Rachel's confidante.*

Notes

"—" interruptions
"/" overlapping dialogue
"..." unfinished or delayed thought

Honoring the punctuation is imperative to navigate the complexity of complicity. Ask questions (?) and make statements (.) that are distinct from one another.

Poor Posturing: A Ten *by Tracey Conyer Lee*

The stage consists of a desk and two chairs. The statue "The Thinker" is projected on to the back wall or is depicted on a large poster that hangs in the room.

Lights up.

Demetrius *is seated at a chair in front of* **Rachel**'s *desk. He leans in eagerly.*

Demetrius   I'm an "A" student. "A." Could I strive for "A+"? Sure. But academic probation?

Rachel   I didn't say "academic." It's just probation.

Demetrius   Like three strikes and I'm serving life?

Rachel   What is that? Sit back, please.

Demetrius   Sit back?

Rachel   Lean back.

Demetrius   Lean back.

Rachel   Back.

Demetrius (*as he does*) Back.

Rachel Ah! Too far.

Demetrius Too far?

Rachel You're slouching.

Demetrius I didn't mean to slouch.

Rachel You shouldn't slouch.

Demetrius How's this?

Rachel Better.

Demetrius Okay.

Rachel How's it feel?

Demetrius How does it feel . . . not to . . . slouch?

Rachel To be upright.

Demetrius Upright.

Rachel Neither aggressive nor lazy.

Demetrius Is that how you see me?

Rachel I think you're fine, Demetrius. It's how you allow—

Demetrius I'm fine, lazy and aggressive.

Rachel Aggressive. Not lazy at all.

Demetrius You find me aggressive right now?

Rachel Now you are upright. In class you are aggressive.

Demetrius Your class?

Rachel I'm sure not only my class.

Demetrius It's a lecture hall. Two hundred-plus students. This may be the most I've ever said in your presence.

Rachel You lean.

Demetrius Lean.

Rachel You lean forward and furrow your brow. It's intimidating.

Demetrius My focus and concentration are intimidating to you?

Rachel You lean and furrow. At me. If you have the desire to be recognized amongst the other—

Demetrius Professor Hobin, I am not naïve to the unlikelihood that you will get to know many of your students. In a class that size, noticing any student is likely based on a negative experience—as is apparently the case here, sadly—but knowing that . . . not being naïve to that . . . my goal in *every* lecture hall in this university is to disappear. To *not* be singled out, targeted, anonymously identified. To take the notes and excel in the work. While my "A" work may not live up to my "A+" potential, my strategy for learning in this environment is to *disappear*. And yet in a sea of faces you find mine intimidating. How is that?

Rachel   You lean and furrow.

Demetrius   Does Jason Simonelli lean and furrow?

Rachel   Who?

Beat.

Demetrius   Am I your only non-academic probationary meeting?

Rachel   Taifus was here earlier.

Demetrius   Tai had a meeting about his lean-and-furrow-note-taking technique?

Rachel   He doesn't lean. He slouches.

Demetrius   He's got an *aggressive* slouch?

Rachel   He's lazy. His grades aren't what yours are.

Demetrius   I thought this wasn't about academics.

Rachel   Don't skirt the issue. I need you to focus.

Demetrius *leans in and furrows (i.e. he focuses).* **Rachel** *approaches him.*

Rachel   See! Right there.

She begins to adjust his body to her satisfaction. It is gentle, but intrusive, like a rape from your favorite uncle. **Cecily** *enters, immediately begins to retreat from what she sees, then proceeds cautiously.*

Rachel   Do you want to graduate? You are better than this, Demetrius.

Demetrius *is physically defiant, but not overwhelming.*

Rachel   I can help you.

She begins to soften the lines and contours of his face. She smooths his brow, lifts the corner of his mouth, etc. **Cecily** *makes her presence known.* **Rachel** *does not flinch.*

Rachel   Yes?

Cecily   Coffee? It's 12:45.

Rachel   Of course! Sorry, Cec. I just need a minute.

Cecily   Ummm . . . Hello, Demetrius. You good?

Demetrius   Hey, Professor Hollingsworth.

Rachel   Cec, would you mind if we pushed back a little? How's your sched?

Cecily   Open, Professor Hobin. Professor Hollingworth's schedule is open.

Rachel   Awesome.

She continues working on **Demetrius**'s *face.*

Cecily   Professor Hobin . . .?

Rachel   We're almost finished here, Cec.

Cecily   Professor.

Rachel   Are you feeling me, Demetrius?

Cecily   Would you like me to stay?

Rachel   Why would I want you to stay?

Demetrius (*escaping her grasp*)   I believe she meant me.

Cecily   With the scrutiny this school is under—

Rachel   Cecily, would you mind just giving us—

Cecily   Professor Hollingsworth!

Rachel   Jesus Christ. Okay. Professor Hollingsworth. We need a moment.

Cecily   Not possible.

Rachel   Why not?

Cecily   Professor Hobin, with Coach Quinn's investigation pending, / I think it best—

Rachel   Arthur is molesting his boys.

Cecily   Allegedly.

Rachel   Allegedly molesting boys with virtually no consequence.

Demetrius   He brings millions of dollars to the university.

Rachel   So he should get away with rape?

Demetrius (*leaning*)   Molestation.

Cecily   Alleged.

Rachel   Which he calls "grooming his team, building winners."

Cecily   We don't know he did anything wrong. But you—

Rachel   We know enough. Rape. Molestation. You're going to argue semantics? They're just words, Ce—they're just words. People need to understand their *actions* / and how they affect others.

Cecily   / Who people? *You* people?

An idea . . . **Rachel** *replicates* **Demetrius***'s focused (leaning) posture.*

Rachel   They better do a thorough investigation. Am I eager? Sure. Demetrius, do you agree?

Demetrius (*leaned in*)   Sure.

Rachel   No! Not eager.

Demetrius *furrows and leans back, legs outstretched and crossed, with his arms folded atop his waist.*

Demetrius   Okay.

Rachel *replicates his new posture.*

Rachel   Maybe he's just misunderstood. Circumspect? (*Re: Herself.*) Yes.

Demetrius   Yes.

Rachel (*Re: Him.*)   No!

Rachel *references the statue of "The Thinker."*

Look at this.

Cecily   What is happening?

Demetrius *adjusts his legs, and leans his chin into his hand replicating the pose of "The Thinker" as he studies it.* **Rachel** *looks disappointed.*

Rachel   Pensive? Absolutely not. These postures when physicalized by you are threats, affronts, and abhorrations. This man is a symbol of great thought and wisdom. If you want to graduate from this institution, you must recognize that thought is equally matched by precept. You must carry a discipline that alleviates the need for any thoughts to occur beyond your own. You must know first. Learn second.

Demetrius   I've never been coached on being a Black man in America by someone so . . . not a Black man.

Rachel   No need to get racial. I taught at an HBCU for seven years. I don't see race.

Cecily   Okay, stop. Demetrius, get your things—

Demetrius   I'm a man, Professor Hollingsworth. I can / handle my business.

Rachel   / I've *been* the minority! I get it. In my case at the HBCU, my Black friends would say "I almost forget you're white sometimes," which may be different for you. You're so Black. No one could miss it. But with me people would forget. Sometimes so did I. / I loved that!

Cecily   / You can't not know you're white.

Rachel   I'd totally forget! It was awesome. Except that everyone kept saying "nigger" around me. "Nigger this, nigger that, nigger, nigger the other thing." All the time. I couldn't believe it. I told them if they didn't stop saying it around me they were going to end up making me say it.

Demetrius   And when you did?

Rachel   Did what?

Demetrius   When you finally *said* "nigger." Because you did say it. I mean, how could you not?

Cecily   You didn't . . . say . . . "n".

Rachel   I would say "n word" if it needed to be said. But all my friends said "nigger" even after I told them they were going to make me say it.

Cecily   You wouldn't say it, no matter how often you heard it, if saying it's not a part of who you are. You blaspheme in front of me all day / everyday. GD JC GD. And it has // never been a struggle for me not to GD. I just don't. /// It's not who I am.

Rachel   / Blaspheme? // What's GD? /// Ohhh shit!

Demetrius & Rachel   "Goddamn!"

Rachel   Oops. Sorry. Come on, Cecily, you never get religious unless—

Cecily   Professor Hollingsworth!

Demetrius   Professor Hollingsworth, she told the niggers what she was going to do. And that's what she did. Why are you mad?

Rachel   It wasn't my fault.

Demetrius   Tah-dow!

Rachel   I asked over and over and they wouldn't respect my wish.

Demetrius   Exactly. She was chomping at the bit for an opportunity to say nigger in front of a bunch of niggers and she finally got it.

Rachel   I was *not* chomping. I'm not some kind of racist. Cecily?

Demetrius   Don't bother. She definitely thinks you're racist.

Rachel   Cecily?

Cecily   I didn't . . .

Demetrius   But now?

Rachel (*with a black Greek step and guttural vocalization. Like, get Que dog on em*)   HBCU, people!

Demetrius (*to* **Cecily**)   You're in the way, Professor Hollingsworth. I'm good. You don't have to stay. Professor Hobin and I have an understanding. Know first. Learn second. I lean and furrow. It's a problem. (*He leans.*) This posture, when physicalized by me is a threat. An affront. An abhorration.

Rachel   Yes! I can help you, Demetrius. Do you want to succeed?

Demetrius   It's the plan. Yes. "If I am to be a thinking member of this university I must recognize that thought is equally matched by precept."

Cecily   Stop it.

Demetrius   "I must carry a discipline that alleviates the need for any thought to occur beyond my own."

Cecily   This is not okay. Tell her what she is doing to you! Tell her!

Demetrius   Know first. Learn second.

Rachel   I'm building winners.

Demetrius   Say it! Know first.

Cecily (*reluctantly.*)   Know first.

Cecily & Demetrius   Learn . . . second.

Rachel   Yaaaaassss! I did it. Good for you, Demetrius.

Demetrius   It's true. It's done.

Rachel   See, Cecily? *You* don't understand.

Cecily   PROFESSOR—

Demetrius   Professor Hollingsworth . . . it's cool. I know you got me, but you can't know what this is.

Rachel   That's your burden.

Demetrius *faces the audience.*

Demetrius   Living or dying while you try is mine.

Lights build hot, then blackout.

Play #7: scholarship babies *by Francisca Da Silveira*

scholarship babies is a cutting examination of educational privilege, affirmative action and what it truly means to go from rags to riches in today's society.

Presented in The Fire This Time Festival Season 10, directed by Kevin R. Free, performed by Cherrye J. Davis (**Felicia**), Jordan Bellow (**Kevin**), and Margaret Ivey (**Leena**).

Characters

Felicia, *mid-twenties, Black, She/Her*
wholesome scholarship baby. the kind that took advantage of every opportunity—
studied abroad in italy, ap classes, not-the-lead-but-got-a-pretty-decent-part-in-the-
musical extracurriculars, track team co-captain.

Kevin, *mid-twenties, Black, He/Him*
passing scholarship baby. like none of his white bro friends knew he was on a
scholarship. they still don't. he's really good at getting them to pay for things.

Leena, *mid-twenties, Black, She/Her*
bitter scholarship baby. she's forever like "fuck these white kids with their bed sheet
vineyard vine clothes and weekend trips to the cape every fucking weekend." she went
home a lot.

Location

boston, ma
seaport district
it's fucking nice
why don't i come here more often? oh yeah
gentrification
principles
but damn look at that view

Setting

present-day american east
the dock leading to one of those fancy spirit boat cruises
a bench with a gold plaque honoring some rich white person's dead wife
a railing

Note

it should smell like seawater and sound like seagulls
we're in new england after all

scholarship babies: a ten-minute play *by francisca da silveira*

present-day american east

A loud cruise ship horn. Like cover your ears loud.

Felicia, **Kevin**, *and* **Leena** *run in.* **Felicia** *wears a really smart blazer/blouse/ high-heel combo.* **Kevin** *wears a suit.* **Leena** *wears some kind of colorful patterned jumpsuit with a matching headscarf done up in a top knot.*

Kevin *and* **Leena** *stop.* **Felicia** *keeps going until she's stopped by the railing gate.*

Leena   THAT SHIT IS LOUD.

Kevin   WHAT?

Leena   THAT SHIT—

The horn stops.

Leena   —is loud. Damn.

Felicia   No.
No no no no no no.

Leena   Sorry, Fee.

Felicia *rounds on* **Kevin** *and begins hitting him.*

Felicia   You stupid idiot!

Kevin   Me? What did I do?

Felicia   If you hadn't gotten us lost, we could have made it.

Kevin   I did not get us lost!

Felicia   As soon as you mentioned the Blue Line, I shoulda known to take your navigation privileges away.

Leena   She's right. Who the hell takes the Blue Line?

Kevin   Nah nah nah. We woulda made it on time if *somebody* hadn't wanted to stop for that blunt.

Leena   FIRST OF ALL. You know it's for my anxiety.

Kevin   Fuck off with that.

Leena Mmm, MMM. See it's people like you that perpetuate Black Stoicism, which continues to undermine the severity and profusion of the deep-seeded mental health issues that children of the African Diaspora face.

Kevin Oh. You're a child of the African Diaspora now?

Leena Nigga, I have always been a child of the African Diaspora.

Kevin Last time I checked you were "Portuguese."

Leena Last time I checked, you were an Oreo. Oh wait. Still are.

Kevin You just have a prejudice against vegans.

Leena Bruh, we literally just ate KFC.

Kevin That shit was my cheat meal.

Leena You're a dumbass.

Felicia Will you both shut up?

Leena And it's not like either of you were saying no.

Beat.

I rest my case.

Kevin Just because you work at a law firm doesn't make you a lawyer.

Leena See, I remember why I never wanted to get high with you when we were in high school. You turn into a paranoid-ass willow tree blowing your shade everywhere.

Kevin You can't blow shade.

Leena Nigga, shut *up*.

Felicia Ya'll both need to SHUT UP.

I'm gonna have a panic attack over here.

She starts to pace. It's annoying in the heels.

So she takes them off and throws them. They land near the bench.

Beat.

Leena Maybe they'll see we're not on the boat and turn back around? Or . . .

*She looks at **Kevin** in a "say something, dumbass" kind of way.*

Kevin Or . . .
Maybe we can ask one of the harbor employees to . . . lend us a smaller boat and we can drive it to the cruise ship and get off and join everyone like we never missed it in the first place.

Felicia and **Leena** *look at him like . . . what?*

Leena I don't know how you ever got into the scholarship program.

Kevin   Cuz I'm charming as fuck.

Felicia   I cannot with you two right now.

Kevin & Leena   Sorry, Fee.

Beat.

Then **Felicia** *starts to laugh. It's kind of manic.*

Kevin   You think we smoked a bad batch?

Leena   Nah, my shit is always clean.

Felicia   I'm screwed. I'm actually screwed. I might as well jump off this thing right now and—

Leena   And what? It's like five feet. All you're gonna do is ruin your blow-out.

Felicia   How the hell am I gonna convince them now?

Leena   Just send an email saying you had a family emergency.

Felicia   That's not good enough.

Leena   They can't fuck with family stuff.

Felicia   It's not good enough. This was my chance.

Kevin   I think you're overreacting.

Felicia *throws a shoe at him. It misses.*

Kevin   You know what. This is why I don't date Black chicks.

Leena   Mmm MMM. Listen, KEVON.

Kevin   It's KEVIN.

Leena   It's about to be my foot up your—

Felicia   I didn't get the grant.

Beat.

Leena   What?

Felicia   The school didn't give me the grant.

Kevin   What do you mean they didn't give you the grant?

Felicia   They just didn't.

Leena   I thought you said—

Felicia   I know. I lied.

Well, no. I didn't lie. I just thought it was a done deal when I applied. But then I got an email saying I was accepted but . . . no money.

Leena   How is that possible? You're like. You're like the epitome of token.

Felicia   I know.

Leena   Like. Out of all of us? Your story beats my deadbeat dad story and Kevin's three thousand brothers and sisters story.

Felicia   I know.

Leena   You like had to swim here.

Felicia   I didn't swim.

Leena   You learned English by reading the McDonald's menu.

Kevin   Shit, I'm hungry.

Leena   We can't even call the rock you're from a third world country. That shit's like fourth.

Felicia   I know, Leena, geeze.

Leena   So how the fuck did you not get the grant? You've gotten every scholarship you ever applied to.

Felicia   Not this one.
I guess I'm not . . .
It doesn't matter anymore. That stuff doesn't matter anymore.

Leena   What stuff?

Felicia   My story. My childhood. It's not my life anymore.

Leena   What the fuck do you mean it's not your life?

Felicia   It's not cute.

Leena   What the FUCK do you mean cute?

Felicia   You know I filled out the FAFSA for the first time in like ten years? It wasn't as scary as I remembered it.

Leena   That's because you're not thirteen doing it alone.

Felicia   Yeah. True. It has this feature now where you can connect it to the IRS and it'll input your tax information. But you know what they didn't ask me for? Any parental stuff. I know I'm twenty-six but. As soon as you hit that grad school option, they're like we don't give a fuck that your parents make like $5 a year. And that because they don't make enough to even buy a mocha frapp from Starbucks, I'm the one pretty much supporting them now. And my aunts and uncles who are still in my fourth world country. So all the FAFSA people and the school see is the salary I make. And it's just enough for them to say I don't need a grant. So here I am. Dressed like Becky with the good hair tryna beg the people who paid for my bourgie boarding school to pay for my bourgie graduate degree at our annual bourgie reunion on a bourgie boat. We never come to this thing. I'm sorry I dragged y'all.

Leena   Don't be sorry. I can sit through four hours of fake laughing with Sarah K. and Sarah M. because it's for you.

Beat.

Felicia   I should just decline the offer.

Leena   Uh no.

Felicia   Yup. I've decided. I'm gonna tell them I can't go anymore.

Leena   Fee.

Felicia   I'll just be a development associate at one non-profit after another for the rest of my life putting together e-newsletters no one ever reads I'll just—

Kevin   NO.

YOU'RE GOING.

Leena   Damn, Kevon, you don't need to yell.

Kevin   Sorry.

But Fee, you got into the school. You have to go.

Felicia   I can't afford it, Kev. They're not giving me the money. And this idea was stupid anyway.

Kevin   You could like. Sue.

Felicia   Sue who?

Kevin   I don't know. The school. The Board of Education? You'd be like Brown. Which is kind of like a metaphor because you are brown.

Beat.

Felicia   Wait. You're right.

Leena   What?

Kevin   I am? Nah, shit, yeah, I am. You not getting this grant must be like. Some kind of affirmative action violation. Right? They are required to make room for people like us. Cuz my dude Obama said so.

Felicia   Shit. I should file a claim. Or start an investigation. Or. Yeah. Threaten to take this to the Board of Education. We'll get everyone to sign a petition.

Kevin   I'll sign that shit twice.

Felicia   We'll get all our rich white boarding school friends on that boat and their rich white parents to sign too. The liberal moms that still wear pussy hats to any and all marches.

Kevin   They'll sign that shit twice!

Felicia   Do you think your law firm could represent me pro-bono? Like if it got to that?

Beat.

Leena? Do you think they'll do it for free if you asked?

Leena   You both must be higher than I thought.

Felicia   I don't think it's even hit me yet.

Leena   It's not the weed that hasn't hit you. We don't have affirmative action anymore.

Kevin   What do you mean we don't have affirmative action? Obama—

Leena   Is not the nigga in charge. Orange dildo and Cruella DeVos got rid of it months ago.

Kevin & Felicia   What?

Beat.

They all sit on the bench.

Leena   That's probably why you didn't get the grant. They're not looking at the full picture. They don't give a shit about your demographics or your personal essay.

Felicia   But.

It was a good essay.

Leena   I bet it was.

Beat.

Felicia   Oh.

Beat.

Then.

Lenna *jumps up.*

Leena   Nah. Fuck that. You know what?

We. Are scholarship babies. Between the three of us, do you know how many rich liberal white people we know? How many board members?

NOPE.

She takes off her shoes.

Leena   We are getting on that boat. And we are getting you that money.

Beat.

They undress.

They run toward the dock. And they get that money.

Section 3

The Shots Heard Round The World: Policing Black Bodies in White America

Arguably the most prominent social issue of the past decade in America has been racism in policing which has led to some of the most heinous and high-profile shootings of innocent, unarmed Blacks. The murder of Trayvon Martin in 2012 thrust the Black Lives Matter movement into the mainstream, setting off a national and global conversation around racial profiling in policing and abuse of power that swelled to a breaking point with the death of George Floyd in the summer of 2020. The conversation around policing, the daily fears of Blacks being accosted or worse for simply being Black, and America's response has literally taken center stage at The Fire This Time over the years. C.A. Johnson's *The Fucking World and Everything in It*, William Watkin's *Black, White, & Blue*, and Jordan Cooper's *Ain't No Mo'* dramatize the myriad ways that the Black community has grappled over the years with the notion that they can be guilty of their own murders by police for simply being Black. Moreover, Natyna Bean's *Assumed Positions* dramatizes the ongoing complicated relationship that Blacks have with choosing a career path in America's policing system.

Foreword by Nia Witherspoon, The Fire This Time Season 7 playwright, whose vast breadth of creative work includes curating Black Art Matters, which focused attention on the critical role of Black arts in Black liberation struggles

We are writing in a state of cosmic imbalance. The stage is our battlefield, laboratory and altar. How do we get there? To the heaven where Black bodies are no longer under attack? To the Black Utopia of our dreams? We write. We witness. We testify. We crack open and dissect. We break harmful ideological patterns that construct us as "monsters." That shapes our lives and deaths. That desecrates our sacredness. Our birthwright of flight and expansion. And our unbridled joy.

My work offers us apertures inside which I hope we can reimagine the imagination. The colonial imagination. The white supremacist capitalist, patriarchal, and heterosexist imagination we have inherited, internalized, and been instructed was normal. I try to offer spaces for us to process traumas inside the indigenous wisdoms we have been disinherited from by law, threat of violation, or denigration.

May we remember how to remember.
May we offer our bodies and spirits rest and restoration.
May we make, receive, and inherit the world we deserve, free of the carceral state.

Play #8: The Fucking World and Everything in It *by C.A. Johnson*

A Black man stands inside a jail cell, while a white cop gazes at him from the other side. Both men have a request: one to be un-cuffed, the other to understand his captive's motives. As tensions mount and their pleas grow more desperate, they must face the inevitability of what comes next and how it is inextricably tied to history.

Presented in The Fire This Time Festival Season 8, directed by Cezar Williams, performed by Sidiki Fofana and Txai Frote.

Characters

Terrance, *male, eighteen, African American.*
Officer Roberts, *male, late twenties, white.*
Officer #2, *male, early thirties, white.*

Setting

The present. An American suburb.

The Fucking World and Everything In It: A Ten-Minute *Play by C.A. Johnson*

A holding cell in a local police station. It is bare besides one stone bench, and a fluorescent light bulb overhead. The bulb is protected by a wire cage that bleeds strange shadows onto the room below.

A long dark hallway on stage right leads out to the rest of the station. Down this corridor we hear the metallic clang of bars opening and closing.

After a moment **Officer Roberts** *enters pushing a handcuffed* **Terrance**. **Roberts** *unlocks the cell, pushes* **Terrance** *inside and locks it behind him.*

Roberts *is a lean man with a kind face, but once the bars close he paces back and forth, deciding his next move.*

Terrance *is a well-built boy who stands erect with a learned pride. He watches* **Roberts**, *guarded.*

After a moment, **Terrance** *gestures with his cuffed hands.*

Terrance   Deese too tight.

Roberts *continues to pace.*

Terrance   Ay man. I said dey too tight.

Roberts   Too bad.

Terrance   You chargin' me with somethin' or what?

Roberts *stops pacing.* **Terrance** *places his cuffed hands between the bars and gestures once more*

Roberts   Not a chance.

Terrance   But I ain't do nothin'.

Roberts   Don't give me that. I saw you. You and that other one standing there up to no good. What were you pushing, huh?

Terrance   See dat? Dat's racial profilin'.

Roberts   No. That's knowing the score.

Terrance   So we competin'?

Roberts   That's right, and I win.

Terrance   Dis is bullshit—

Roberts   Watch your mouth, boy.

Terrance   I ain't yuh boy. Let's get dat straight.

Roberts   Oh, don't you—don't twist my words like that. Don't make this one of those—things—you got me? Just save us both a whole lotta trouble, and tell me what you were up to.

Terrance   Not without no lawyer. And judgin' by dat dere uniform you ain't no detective so . . .

He fiddles with his handcuffs uncomfortably.

Roberts   I'm an officer of the law. I can help you.

Terrance   Dat's what you call helpin' me? What happened out dere?

Roberts   You were mouthing off—

Terrance   I was axin' a question! "Hands up," you said. And I'm jus wonderin' what I do wrong. Me and my boy jus standin' dere sippin' some cokes.

Roberts   And then your *boy* ran—

Terrance   You wuz standin' dere witcho hand on yo piece—

Roberts   That's my job. I investigate suspicious behavior.

Terrance   So havin' me a cold drink is suspicious?

Roberts   When you do so on street corners in packs, yes. Yes it is.

Terrance   Cool. I be sure to pass dat message along.

His fiddling is more pronounced now.

Roberts   Listen, smart ass, I want to know what you were selling.

Terrance   Look, man. I ah'ready told you. Get me a civil defenda and we cuh talk. Othawise . . .

He holds his gaze for a moment, but is distracted by the handcuffs.

He's in pain.

Roberts *has an idea. He pulls a key ring from his waste, and dangles it in the air between them. He looks from the keys to* **Terrance**, *not in a sadistic manner, but with more apprehension than anything else.*

Roberts   Just tell me what was going on, huh. Tit for tat?

A pause.

Terrance   Nuthin was goin' on. Me and my boy wuz sittin' on the corner of Birch like alwayz sippin' some sodas. Hollin' at the ladies. Mindin' ours. Den you roll up, gun cocked accusin' a nigga uh somethin'.

Roberts   That's not everything. I need to know everything.

Terrance   Aight. Let's see . . . I woke up dis mornin' round 9:30 and my manz text me. Said he want grab subs from M & T's so we linked up. You cuh check my phone and errything. Got to the spot, Miles ordered the sandwiches and I paid for da cokes. Den we waited outside for our order. Boom. You showed up.

Roberts   Miles, huh? And your name is?

Terrance   Shit.

Roberts   Don't let me stop you.

Terrance   Nah, I'm done.

Roberts   Tell me more about you and this Miles. How long you been partners?

Terrance *is silent.*

Roberts   Look, bud. Once those detectives get a hold you, you're mincemeat. So you might as well tell me the truth.

Terrance   Right. So you cuh help me?

Roberts   So I can help both of us!

Terrance *shrugs.*

Roberts   Listen you—ugh—you were up to something. And I caught you in the act. Only problem is, I need more information to nail your ass to the wall. So give me what I need!

Terrance   So much fuh dat help.

Roberts *is enraged by this. He uses the keys to open the cell door. He advances towards* **Terrance** *who backs quickly away into a corner. The two men breathe right into each other's faces.*

Roberts   How about now? Wanna talk?

Roberts *grabs* **Terrance** *by the collar, and shakes him.*

Roberts   Just spit it out!

Terrance *says nothing, and* **Roberts** *loosens his grip. He takes a few, uneven steps backward.* **Terrance** *stays put.*

Roberts   Wrong move, kid. People like you . . . you need people like me. I'm just trying to weed out the truth of things. Just trying to . . .

He trails off.

Terrance   Jus . . . at lease let me call my mom's. (**Roberts** *doesn't respond.*) Please? I get a phone call.

Roberts (*he hasn't even heard* **Terrance**)   Just tell me who you are and maybe—

Terrance   Terrance, aight? My name is Terrance Haywood. My mom's is Rita Mae Haywood and Benny Coons my pops. No use lookin' up old Benny cuz I ain't seen 'em in ten years, but Mom is prolly blowin' up my phone as we speak. She got a bad hip. I'm s'posed to take her to da doctor at 2. I got three brothas upstate, armed robbery, two of 'em. Da other one been a addict since da day I was born. And me . . . my C average got me cross da stage jus fine. But let's be real, all dat don't matter, do it? Not da way you lookin' at me.

Roberts   You don't know what I'm thinking okay.

Terrance   Don't I?

A pause. **Roberts** *shakes his head vigorously, as if trying to wake himself.*

Terrance   tol'dju all of it. I'm innocent.

The light bulb overhead flickers.

Roberts   No. You . . . you were up to something. If I can just prove it. Right now. All this'll blow over. I turned the corner and there you were, you and Miles. Yes, Miles. And you were holding cokes, but from where I was standing it could've been anything. And you . . . the way you were looking at me. Right in my eyes. So fucking bold. And the other one takes off and you're still talking and you're hands are up but I'm trying to focus on two things at once, and my walkie is on my waist, and . . . you moved. Why'd you have to move?

Terrance   My phone.

Roberts (*remembering*)   Your phone . . .

He stares off for a moment, humming a tune, most likely the ringtone. After a few notes he shakes his head vigorously, willing himself back to this moment. Desperate now.

Just tell me what you were doing on that corner.

Terrance   I already tol'dju. Waitin' on a sanwich.

Roberts There's so fucking many of you. How am I supposed to tell the difference? How am I supposed to do my job? You know, yesterday my son turned one. And it was a good party, Terrance. Really it was. Then today comes . . . and you on that corner . . . looking me right in the eyes . . .

A pause.

Terrance I was terrified.

Roberts But I was scared too.

Terrance Only yo scared was holdin' a gun.

The light bulb overhead flickers.

Roberts Well, no. No. You and me are standing there, sure, but it's the behavior. Don't stand on corners, Terrance. Don't hang out with guys who run from cops, holding cokes that could be guns for all I know. Just don't fucking do that. Stay . . . Jesus just stay indoors.

Terrance Not goin' nowhere? Not bein' nobody?

Roberts I never said that. I—

The abrupt clang of bars locking and unlocking once more. **Roberts** *startles. He turns toward the sound.*

Another **Officer** *enters from the hall.*

Officer #2 Roberts. What're you doing back here? It's time.

Roberts Of course. Right. I'm ready.

Officer #2 I hope so. Turns out the kids got no record, not even a goddamn in-school suspension. But don't you worry about that. We'll dig something up.

Roberts *sits on the bench.*

Officer #2 This shit happens, brother.

Roberts The way he looked at me . . .

Officer #2 Trust me I know it. Like they own the whole fucking world and everything in it. Well, guess what? They don't. And we don't owe them shit. You did your job.

Roberts I did my job.

A pause.

Officer #2 Look, I'm gonna give you a minute to pull yourself together, alright? (*Starts to go, but thinks better of it.*) Just think of Laura and Nicholas, then smile for the camera.

He exits

A pause. **Roberts** *sits on the bench.*

Roberts   You're not really here.

Terrance   Not anymore. No.

Roberts   Right.

The light bulb overhead flickers.

Terrance *sits as well, in a position nearly identical to* **Roberts**.

For a moment, they might even be the same man.

Terrance   He's wrong you know. You owe me everything.

A very long, possibly awkward pause.

The light bulb overhead flickers once, then twice, and just as we expect a third . . .

Play #9: Black, White, & Blue *by William Watkins*

A Black motorist. A white cop. A bystander who is far from innocent. Which truth will you believe? *Black, White, & Blue* explores the deadly stereotypes that make us all slaves to fear.

Presented in The Fire This Time Festival Season 9, directed by Candis C. Jones, performed by Kambi Gathesha (**Jerome**), Kevin Neccai (**Bill**), and Ashley Ortiz (**Director**).

Characters

Jerome, *Black male, twenties to forties, an actor.*
Bill, *white male, twenties to forties, an actor.*
Director, *female, any age, not Black, not white.*

Time

Now.

Place

A stage.

Black, White, & Blue: A Play in One Act *by William Oliver Watkins*

Red, white, and blue flashing lights.

Jerome *sits in a chair center stage, staring straight ahead and holding a steering wheel with both hands. After a moment,* **Bill**, *wearing a police uniform, saunters casually onto the stage with his hands on his hips. He walks to stand next to* **Jerome***'s chair.*

Bill   Evening, sir. Did you know one of your brake lights was out?

Jerome   Oh, sorry, Officer. I didn't realize.

Bill   Yeah, yeah, ya gotta stay on top of that kinda stuff, man. Do ya happen to have your license and registration on ya?

Jerome   Uh, yes sir I do, Officer. They're in the glove compartment.

He reaches for the glove compartment. **Bill** *whips out his gun and points it at* **Jerome**.

Bill   SIR! DO NOT MOVE! DON'T MOVE! DON'T MOVE!

Jerome *holds his hands up toward* **Bill** *to say . . .*

Jerome   WAIT!

Bill *jerks the gun as he mimes kickback. With each jerk,* **Jerome** *mimes taking a bullet to the chest.*

Bill   BUP! BUP! BUP! BUP! BUP!

Director (*offstage*)   Stop please! Mark, can we get the works?!

Work lights come on. The **Director** *walks onto the stage from the audience.*

Director   Jerome, relax for a sec?

Jerome *gets up, stretches, maybe checks his phone.*

Director   Okay, so right now, it's playing like you just shoot him out of the blue.

Bill   Yeah, I felt that. It feels like one minute I'm asking for his ID and then the next . . . I shoot him. So, I guess I'm just not understanding my motivation here.

Director   Okay . . . I think it's about stakes. What do you know about this guy? Not much. Is he a gang member? An addict? You don't know. You make a mistake here, this could be your *Last. Day. On. Earth.* Yeah? Okay! Let's try it again and this time, just make it more important, you know. Raise the stakes.

She walks back out into the audience. The men return to their starting positions.

Director (*offstage*)   Alright everybody, once again!

Work lights go out. Red, white, and blue lights come on.

Bill (*colder and meaner*)   Evening, sir. Are you aware your brake light's busted?

Jerome   Sorry, Officer, I wasn't.

Bill   License and registration.

Jerome   It's in the glove compartment. I'll just—

He reaches. **Bill** *pulls his gun.*

Bill   SIR! DON'T MOVE! DON'T MOVE!

Jerome   Wait! You asked me to—

Bill *mimes shooting.* **Jerome** *mimes getting hit.*

Bill   BUP! BUP! BUP! BUP! BUP!

Director   WORKS!

The work lights come on. The **Director** *comes onto the stage.*

Bill, great adjustment. I wanna work with Jay for a sec, go grab a coffee.

Jerome (*playful*)　And a donut, bitch.

Bill (*playful, middle finger*)　You have the right to blow me.

He leaves the stage.

Director　Okay so you're making some great choices, but right now I'm not really seeing *why* Bill shoots you. He just . . . does it.

Jerome　Uhhhh . . . that's not what happens?

Director　Well, *on the page*, yes. But this officer pulls you over for a minor traffic violation and ends up putting five bullets into you, so . . .

Jerome　So, what?

Director　What I'm saying is: if we assume that this officer has been trained for this kind of a situation . . .

Jerome　Uh-huh.

Director　Then the only reason for him to draw his weapon at all . . .

Jerome　Uh-huh.

Director　. . . let alone fire shots . . .

Jerome　Uh-huh.

Director　Is if *you* do something *wrong* first.

Jerome *looks at the* **Director** *for a long moment. Finally . . .*

Jerome　Uh-huh. Well . . . I'm not entirely sure I agree with that.

Director　Hey, don't take my word for it. The data backs me up. I mean, how many of these types of shootings have there been in just the past few years alone and there've been how many convictions? Not a lot, right? So . . . you know? Do the math.

Jerome　I just, I think it's more complicated than that.

Director　Look, Jerome. I don't wanna get into a philosophical debate with you. We don't have the time. But for the sake of this piece, it is very important that we honor *both* of these characters' points of view. And the way you're playing this right now, it's coming off very one-sided. Bill's *cop* is coming off as the bad guy here and your *shooting victim* is coming off as, well, a victim. And I don't believe in "bad guys" and "victims." It's lazy storytelling, know what I mean?

Jerome　What would you suggest?

Director　Let's try it again and this time give it a little more of an . . . "urban" quality.

Jerome　Urban?

Director　Yeah, play it with a little more attitude.

Jerome   Attitude.

Director   And feel free to improvise.

Jerome   Improvise?

Director   Yeah, like, your subtext is like . . .

She assumes the demeanor of a stereotypical thug.

"Aww, shit! Here we go again! Dis honky muthafucka pullin' over another Black man for no gott-damn reason!"

She becomes herself again.

Obviously not like that cause I'm a horrible actor, but you get the point, yes?

Jerome   Right. But the dialog is taken from the transcript of an actual incident, so . . .?

Director   So . . .?

Jerome   What about . . . the truth?

Director   What truth? Whose truth? How do you define truth? "Truth" is a concept. It has no mass. No volume.

Jerome *is speechless.*

Director   Look. If they want the transcript, they can go to YouTube and get it. We're making theater. Yes?

Jerome   Right.

Director   Great!

Jerome *sits down in his chair with a slouching lean. He puts one hand on the steering wheel and the other on his crotch.*

Director   Exactly! Excellent adjustment, Jerome! Bill! We need you back, buddy!

Bill *jogs into position. The* **Director** *returns to the audience.*

Director (*offstage*)   Once more, folks! Bill, *stakes*! Jerome, *attitude*! Mark, lights please!

Red, white, and blue pulsing flashes. **Bill** *approaches* **Jerome**.

Bill   Sir, do you know why I pulled you over this evening?

Jerome   No, "Officer," I do not.

Bill   Your tail light is out.

Jerome *shrugs nonchalantly.*

Bill   Is this your vehicle, sir?

Jerome (*under his breath*)   I'm drivin' it ain't I?

Bill   What did you say?

Jerome (*fake white guy voice*)   I said, "It certainly is, Officer."

Bill   License and registration.

Jerome *raises his hands slowly.* **Bill** *tenses but he keeps his pistol holstered.* **Jerome** *places both hands slowly on the steering wheel.*

Bill   What are you doing?

Jerome   Staying alive, Officer. By any means necessary.

Bill *looks out into the audience for help. Nothing.*

Bill   Sir, I need you to give me your license and registration.

Jerome   I ain't taking my hands offa this wheel.

Bill   License and registration! NOW!

Jerome   I AIN'T TAKING MY FUCKIN' HANDS OFF THIS FUCKIN' WHEEL!

Bill *turns out to the audience and throws his hands up, exasperated.*

Director (*offstage*)   WHY ARE YOU STOPPING?!

Bill   He's not *doing* anything. If he doesn't *do* anything, then I can't shoot him.

The **Director** *leaps up onto the stage.*

Director (*whiny baby voice*)   "If he doesn't *do* anything, then I can't *shoot* him." (*Regular voice.*) *How* are you not *getting* this?! This is not about what *he* does. This is about what *you* do! Back to one!

The actors take their initial positions. **Bill** *comes out from backstage.*

Director   Bill, what's going through your mind right now? Maybe this is just a regular guy who happens to be Black. Or *maybe* this is one o' dem stone cold, glock-toting *niggaz* they talk about in the rap songs.

Jerome *starts to stand up in protest.*

Bill   SIR! DO NOT EXIT THE VEHICLE!

Jerome *sits rigidly back down.*

Director   Good! Good, Bill! Use what he gives you!

Bill *slowly approaches* **Jerome**'s *"car window."*

Bill   Evening, sir. Do you know why I pulled you over?

Jerome *turns to look at* **Bill**.

Jerome   You don't have to do this.

Director   FOCUS! Don't listen to him. We're talking about a man . . . did I say man? No. Not a man. This is a *beast* who has been genetically engineered for generations to have superior strength and speed and endurance. Why else would you need to shoot him *five times*?

Jerome *burns with fear and rage.* **Bill** *is paralyzed by tension.*

Director   No. No, this thing is not human. THIS IS AN *ANIMAL*. This ANIMAL has suffered persecution and oppression at the hands of a system in which he has no real voice. The very system that you have sworn to protect and serve with your life. AND HE *HATES* YOU FOR THAT. He hates you and everything thing you stand for! And if you give him half a chance, he is going to BLOW YOUR FUCKING BRAINS OUT. Don't give him that chance!

Jerome *grips the "steering wheel" as if his life depends on it.*

Jerome   I don't have a weapon. How can I be a threat?

Director   Is this a law-abiding citizen? Or is this the predator who's about to widow your wife? Orphan your kids?

Jerome   I DON'T. HAVE. A GUN.

Director   Maybe he does. Maybe he doesn't. You have SECONDS to make that call, Bill. DO YOU HEAR ME?! SECONDS! SO MAKE. THEM. COUNT.

Jerome   You have all the time you want. You pulled *me* over.

Bill   One of your brake lights is out.

Jerome   Look at me. *See* me. I am a man. I am a son. I am a brother. Just like you.

Bill   License and registration?

Jerome   I refuse to play a badly written character in a script I didn't write. I refuse to be another sacrifice on the altar of bigotry.

Bill   I'm afraid. Everyone is watching me. Scrutinizing my every move.

Jerome   That's why you have to STAND UP. YOU have the *GUN*. YOU have the *POWER*. I DON'T UNDERSTAND WHY YOU HAVE TO DO THIS! WHY YOU *KEEP* DOING THIS!

Director   *STAY ON SCRIPT!*

Jerome   WE STAY ON SCRIPT AND I DIE!

Bill   WE STAY ON SCRIPT AND HE DIES!

The **Director** *walks to* **Bill***, pulls the pistol out of his holster and puts it in his hands.*

Director   You have to do this because it's what happened. You have to do this because it's the truth.

Jerome   Whose truth?

Director   Whoever's left alive.

The **Director** *moves* **Jerome** *like a puppet into the position of reaching for the glove compartment. He is powerless to stop her. She then positions* **Bill** *to point his gun at* **Jerome**.

Director　Say the lines.

Jerome　Do this and your life will never be the same.

Director　Say the lines.

Bill (*painful, fighting*)　No!

The **Director** *takes the gun from* **Bill**'s *hand and points it at his head.*

Director　Don't take my word for it. The data backs me up. It's him or you. Choose wisely. If it were me, I'd say the lines.

Bill (*giving in*)　SIR! DO NOT MOVE! DON'T MOVE! DON'T MOVE!

Director　Excellent adjustment.

The **Director** *puts the gun back in* **Bill**'s *hand and points it at* **Jerome**.

Jerome (*desperate defiance*)　I AM AN AMERICAN CITIZEN! I AM A HUMAN BEING! I DESERVE RESPECT! I WILL NOT STAY SILENT WHILE YOU SHOOT MY PEOPLE DOWN LIKE DOGS!

The men are locked in this position: **Jerome** *forever reaching for his ID,* **Bill** *forever aiming his gun. They are trapped in an eternal Mexican standoff.*

Lights begin to fade. Spotlight on the **Director** *as she walks to the front of the stage and speaks directly to us.*

Director　How are we still not getting this?

Blackout.

Play #10: Ain't No Mo' *by Jordan E. Cooper*

A small church holds an earth-shattering funeral on the election night of America's first Black president.

Presented in The Fire This Time Festival Season 8, directed by Cezar Williams, performed by Jordan E. Cooper, Patrice Bell, Karen Chilton, Sidiki Fofana, Txai Frote, Maurice McRae, and Eliana Pipes.

Characters

Pastor Freeman, *a hopeful and fiery Black man of the past and present.*
Church Folk, *a congregation of grieving Black folk.*

Ain't No Mo' *by Jordan E. Cooper*

Lights slowly rise up. 11 p.m. November 4, 2008. In a small church somewhere between Heaven and Hell. An organ begins to play "Soon I Will Be Done." We see pallbearers carrying a casket down the center of the audience onto the stage. They are followed by weeping mourners, most of whom are screaming at the top of their lungs, falling on the floor, etc . . . you know how we do. Once the casket is set, each member of the community passes by to view the body, with **Pastor Freeman** *being the last to view. He closes the casket and marches up to the pulpit. We hear the faint sound of a gunshot or a car back firing. He subtly reacts, until he quickly reads the room and notices no one else heard it.*

Freeman   Good evenin', chuch.

Church Folk   Evening.

Freeman   I said good evenin', chuch.

Church Folk   Evenin'.

Freeman   We are gathered here today to put asunder one whom many of you know, one whom many of us have known our entire lives. Today, we give to the dirt of the earth our beloved brother and friend "Righttocomplain." Brother lived a good and fruitful life and was a devoted member to the African American community. He had many mothers and fathers, and too many children with too many mothers to even begin to count, yes, brother "Righttocomplain" was just a little loved like that. This man, this brother, this force lived a great life until he was murdered by a recent major event . . .

Church Folk   Hmm.

Freeman   As this night of our lord November 4th Two Hundred Thousand and Eight, our beloved brother was beaten, sodomized, and murdered by the election of the First Negro President of these United States. On this night of November 4th Two Hundred Thousand and Eight we lost an asset . . . a pillar of our community. But this night is what I would call a bittersweet night . . . we know that we are all hurt and battered by the death of our dear brother on this night but also . . . on this night of November 4th Two Hundred Thousand and Eight, we mark the death of our suffering as people in this wretched land. On this night, I can't help but see being pushed to the forefront the fact that all of our blood shed along the streets, woods, alleys, and waters of this country did not shed in vain. And by the grace of God, with the death of our suffering comes the death of our anger, our attitude, our ability to never be satisfied with the progress that has been made within this land. Today . . . is a sad day, a day some of us would have never even dared to dream, a day where all sins of inequality, injustice, and ignorance will forever be washed away. After today, we will have no reason to ever walk around with the weight of our ancestors' tears guiding our face down to the ground. After today, We may now name our children Tyquamotrin and MonaLisaKeishawanda in peace, without a giggle . . . or a sneer. For as of now, the leader of this country is . . . Black . . . Light skinned to be exact.

Church Folk   Hmm . . . my, my, my.

Freeman   Now I know you're hurt, and you're in pain, we're all in pain, but we have to see what God wants us to see in this time of tragedy. Brother will be the last of the negro saints that has to march in through that dark and bloody back door. I know we're gonna miss him but we have to realize that with his absence we are in a far better position, listen to me now. I said our president, the leader of this recently free world is . . . (*silent*) Black . . . Light skinned to be exact, therefore he knows and-and-and-and-and-and he sees, and he sympathizes with us all, he is a friend who will travel the world and back again, his heart is true, he is a pal and a confidant . . . he-he-he-he-he- is . . . he is . . . my nigga.

And if we threw a party and invited EVERYONE we knew, we would see, that the biggest batch of Kool-Aid would be from him and the card attached would say "Thank you for being my friend" . . . And when the president of these United States is your friend, yo nigga, yo goon . . . things change. After today, we may now walk into a Kentucky Fried Chicken and order a Five Dollar Fill-Up with an original two-piece leg and thigh, wedge fries, and a biscuit, without wondering if Little Joey thinks we ALL like Five Dollar Fill-Up's with an original two-piece leg and thigh, wedge fries, and a biscuit. Why? Because the president is WHAT? Yo. Nigga . . . I want you to sit BACK and WATCH the chains begin to roll off you like water on a feathered wing. WATCH how the atmosphere begins to shift, and mold, and change into a land where you REAP the benefits of your leader being yo nigga. After your leader is yo nigga, can't can't can't can't can't can't can't nobody use the word nigga like niggas can use the word nigga! We own it, "Nigga" is our slave . . . our property, paid for with cotton, sex, and sweat. After today, you will only hear it out of the mouths of its owners because the president is WHAT? Yo nigga. The next time you see the K.K.K. you can now boldly say F.U.C.K you . . . them . . . they . . . it . . . Yell it out yo' soul with a mighty rush of fire and an awesome rage of wind, we may now say FUCK it. Yes I said fuck, don't act like you ain't never felt a fuck in your spirit, come on now somebody . . . because the president is a nigga there ain't no mo' discrimination, ain't no mo' holleration, ain't gone be NO more haterration in this dancerie, do you hear me what I say? I say it ain't no mo'.

The atmosphere begins to shift. We hear a faint gunshot, only heard by **Pastor Freeman***; he manages to ignore it.*

Ain't no mo' blueish red light in the rear-view mirror when you taking your family to the church picnic and all you got in yo trunk is three Dollar Store aluminum pans of sister thread gill's chitlins, cornbread, and collard greens. Ain't no mo' waiting for FEMA while the Louisiana sun is stabbing at yo back on the interstate and your grandmama is backstroking in a river of expired bodies. Ain't no mo' massa' tip toein' in yo' mama's room to rock the shack into the midnight hour. Ain't no mo' shot down dreams with its blood soaking the concrete outside room 306. Ain't no mo' riots. Ain't no mo' Rosewood. Ain't no mo' Jasper. Ain't no mo' Jiggin'. Ain't no mo' Shufflin'. Ain't no mo' Shuckin'. Ain't no mo' Amos. Ain't no mo Andy. Ain't no mo Emmit Till. Ain't no mo' Rodney King. Ain't no mo Jena 6. Ain't no mo' Stop. Ain't no mo' Frisk. Ain't no mo' getting followed around by the tall white lady in the K-Mart on Jones street. There ain't no mo' double locking they car when you walk by, they thinking you gonna hot wire they car and drive it out the parking lot, when they know they just saw you pulling up in car they can't even afford. That's all over . . . that's all done. I know we sad to see a mighty soldier march on to glory, but we must not forget that with his death comes birth of our savior, our leader, our rock in the puddle, our way when there ain't no way, our rumble in the jungle, our Huxtable in the crack house. As we lay to rest our "Righttocomplain" we shall WAKE UP our new life. In this new life there ain't no mo' strife, no more marches to be led and no more tears to be shed because the president is WHAT? (*Beat.*) I guess ya'll done went to sleep on Pastor Freeman, I-I-I-I-I must be preaching to myself this evening cause I ain't heard a shout yet. I said there ain't no more tears to be shed because the president is WHAT? Ain't no more marching in the streets to be heard, because the president is WHAT? Come on and say it somebody, I can see the spirit doing the Cupid Shuffle in yo chest right now, waiting to rise up and reveal itself as yo true voice . . . I want every colored person in this room to turn to yo neighbor and say neighbor . . . The president is my nigga . . . Louder . . . SAY THE PRESIDENT IS MY NIGGA . SAY IT AGAIN, THE PRESIDENT IS MY NIGGA . . . THE PRESIDENT IS MY NIGGA . . . THE PRESIDENT IS MY NIGGA . . . THE PRESIDENT IS *THE* NIGGA, HA! . . . THE PRESIDENT IS *A* NIGGA, HA! . . . THE PRESIDENT IS A NIGGA . . . THE PRESIDENT IS A NIGGA . . . THE PRESIDENT . . . is yo nigga . . .

Gunshot.

WATCH THAT NIGGA DO IT!

Church Folk   Yeah!

Freeman   I SAY WATCH THAT NIGGA DO IT!

Church Folk   Yeah, yeah!

Freeman   CAN I GET AN AMEN?

Church Folk   AMEN!

Freeman   CAN I GET A CHAKA KHAN?

Church Folk   CHAKA KHAN!

Freeman   CHAKA KHAN, CHAKA KHAN! (*Singing.*) Because when I think of my nigga . . . (*Music starts.*) and what he'll do for me. When I think of my nigga, and how he'll set us free . . . I can dance, dance, dance, dance, dance all night. Come on somebody. . . . (*Praise music sets into tempo.*) I said when I think of my nigga, what he'll do for me.

When I think of my nigga, how he'll set me free . . . I can dance, dance, dance, dance, dance, dance, dance, all night . . . Glory to God! Hey! I said—

Church Folk (*singing*)   When I think of my nigga, what he'll do for me. When I think of my nigga, how he'll set me free . . . I can dance, dance, dance, dance, dance, dance, dance, all night . . .

*The **Church Folk** begin to dance like David danced.*

Freeman   DANCE!

*Gunshot. Distant enough that **Freeman** can still ignore it.*

Church Folk   DANCE!

Scream.

Freeman   DANCE!

Gunshot.

Church Folk   DANCE!

Siren.

Freeman   DANCE! DANCE!

Chanting crowd.

Church Folk   DANCE! DANCE!

Gunshot.

Freeman   DANCE! DANCE!

Gunshot.

Church Folk   DANCE! DANCE!

Gunshot.

Freeman   YA'LL DON'T WANNA HAVE NO CHURCH IN HERE!

*The atmosphere begins to shift. A spirit has consumed the entire room. The **Church Folk** dance, shout, praise, and sing. **Pastor Freeman** leads this shift until he begins to hear the sounds of gunshots and sirens that he is no longer able to ignore, as they attempt to overtake the sound of celebration. We begin to hear the sound of news reports build on top of each other, stating the deaths of those like Oscar Grant,*

Aiyana Jones, Trayvon Martin, Rekia Boyd, Jordan Davis, Alton Sterling, Philando Castille, the Charleston Nine, and countless others. **Pastor Freeman** *is the only one who hears this chaos; it freezes him. The* **Church Folk** *continue to dance, shout, praise, and sing. We now sit in an overwhelming atmosphere of gunshots, blood, news reports, screams, speeches, and sirens. He looks out, consumed. He is full but somehow completely empty. The* **Church Folk** *continue to dance, shout, praise, and sing around his emptiness. Lights fade to black.*

Play #11: Assumed Positions *by Natyna Bean*

During the first night in her new home, Naya discovers how easily a little distance can create a huge impact. When she finds herself arrested by the sudden shifts of someone she previously believed to know even better than herself, she is faced with the conundrum of whether or not she is willing—or able—to get to know this newfound stranger.

Presented in The Fire This Time Festival Season 11, directed by Ebony Noelle Golden, performed by Antu Yacob (**Matcha**) and Linda LaBeija (**Naya**).

Assumed Positions: A Short Play *by Natyna Bean*

West Philadelphia. Present day. Night.

A dimly lit, nearly empty living room. Half-opened boxes litter the floors. An Ikea futon is positioned in the center of the room.

Matcha, *twenty-seven, dressed in all black, enters wielding a gun and badge.*

Matcha   Anybody home?

Naya (*off*)   Who's asking?

Matcha *sticks the gun in the back of their pants.*

Matcha   Officer Davis. I'm responding to a call about a possible B and E to this here residence.

Naya (*off*)   Nope. No calls here.

Matcha   Hmm. That's funny. Are you sure no calls were made / from this location?

Naya (*off*)   I assure you no calls were made. Try next door. They might have a landline. My partner and I don't own one. I certainly made no calls and she isn't / home yet—

Matcha   She? Excuse me, miss. Did you say "she"?

Naya (*off*)   She. And/or they. But I wouldn't expect you to know / nothing 'bout that—

Matcha   Oh, so you're one of those?

Naya (*off*)   One of those what, officer?

Matcha   One of those . . . Janelle Monae types?

Naya (*off*)   Can't see how any of that is your busi–do you have a warrant for this uh . . . intrusion?

Matcha   I can't say I do.

Naya (*off*)   Oh, the irony.

Matcha   How's that?

Naya (*off*)   Well, considering ain't nobody here make a phone call. And you have found yourself here, in my home, with no warrant. Seems to me that you're the one doing the breaking and entering.

Matcha   Are you sassing me, miss?

Naya (*off*)   I'm just stating facts, officer.

Matcha   Well, how's this for a fact? You're all alone. With me. And only one of us has a gun.

Naya (*off*)   Now, is any of that / necessary?

Matcha   Come out, with your hands held high.

Naya (*off*)   Excuse me?

Matcha   I said, come out. With your hands. Held high.

Naya (*off*)   How high?

Matcha   High enough for me to see everything.

Naya (*off*)   . . . Everything?

Matcha   Evuhreethang.

Naya (*off*)   Ohhhhkay.

Naya (*twenty-seven*) *enters hands up, wearing overalls, a lace bra, and a faux look of fear.*

Matcha   Oh, that's not gonna do.

Naya   I'm sorry, officer. Are you gonna arrest me?

Keeping her hands up, she dramatically turns around, arches her back, and pokes out her butt.

Matcha   Only if you don't comply.

Naya   Well, what is it that you want me to do?

They hook the badge onto their shirt and slowly walks towards **Naya**. *They spin* **Naya** *around.*

Matcha   For one: I recall telling you that I wanted to see everything.

Naya *allows* **Matcha** *to undo the suspenders.*

Naya   Is that all . . . officer?

Matcha *lowers* **Naya**'s *hands down. They fall around* **Matcha**'s *neck.*

Matcha   Close your eyes.

Naya   What else?

Matcha   Tilt your head back.

Naya *complies.* **Matcha** *begins to decorate* **Naya**'s *neck with light, gentle kisses.*

Naya   Mmm. You remembered.

Matcha   Of course. You really think I'd forget?

Naya   It's been a while.

Matcha   Not long enough. This neck? This spot? I'll always remember how I conquered you.

Naya   Conquered, huh?

Matcha   Brought you down like my mouth was a trumpet and you were the walls of Jericho.

Naya   But, conquered? That's the word we going with?

Naya *pulls back.* **Matcha** *holds on.*

Matcha   You right. Too . . . militaristic. How about, my kisses. On this neck. On this very spot of the neck . . . is the key to your kingdom.

Naya   My kingdom, huh?

Matcha   Mmhmm.

Matcha *stops. Waits for* **Naya**'s *rating.*

Naya   Better.

Matcha   [Yes!] How was the ride from the airport? I'm so sorry I couldn't grab you.

Naya   Matcha, it's fine. I found the key in the mailbox like you told me to and just let myself—

Matcha   Hmm, you smell so good.

Naya   Course, I do. I couldn't greet my baby smelling like yesterday now could I? Hopped in the shower soon as I could. Fourteen-hour flight has a way of trapping in a funk nobody deserve to smell. Let alone wear.

Matcha   I just can't believe you're here.

Places it on the coffee table.

Naya   That thing looks pretty heavy.

Matcha   You wear it enough, you get used to it. Now that thing right there.

Naya *looks around.*

Naya   What thing?

She notices **Matcha** *watching her ass.*

Matcha   Thing look like you ain't waste not one meal while you was down there.

Naya   Shut up.

Matcha   Nah, I like it. I like it a lot.

Matcha *lifts* **Naya** *and carries her to the futon. As* **Matcha** *goes to remove her shirt,* **Naya** *considers* **Matcha**'*s badge.*

Naya   O shxt.

Matcha   What? . . . Baby, what?

Naya   This is . . . real?

Matcha   Yeah, it's real. What you think I was—

Naya   I thought you were wearing a very realistic prop.

I thought maybe you were flexing with your role-play, I don't know.

Matcha (*small laugh*)   Flexing.

Naya   Is that silly of me?

Matcha   No, but I did tell you that I had a surprise for you / when you returned.

Naya   Yeah, you did say you had a surprise. I was expecting like a puppy or a new tattoo. Jewelry maybe, but whoa. Wow.

She considers the badge like a fossil.

Matcha   Say something, Naya.

Naya   I just need a moment / to take this all—

Matcha   What did you think I was doing all this time?

Naya   Matcha, you said you were enrolled in a criminal justice program.

Matcha   I was.

Naya   The academy is not just a program, Matcha. But okay. It's a lot to swallow but . . . Okay.

Matcha   Is it really okay?

Naya   . . . Let's just give it a sec for it to settle. / Let it digest.

Matcha   I don't want the settled words. I want the raw shxt.

Naya   I want to be intentional with my words. They won't matter / if I'm not intentional.

Matcha   Naya. Could you just give it to me raw? Intentionally.

Naya   . . . Nope. Let's enjoy the night. We can leave it for later.

She sets the badge down. **Matcha** *retrieves it.*

Matcha   You acting like you don't know me.

Naya   . . . Were there were no other options? Fire-fighting?

Matcha What's so bad about this, Naya? Other than what you think you know about us.

Naya Us. Oh, dear. Nope, not a dream. / Us . . . Us.

Matcha I would like to know how this is specifically impacting you.

Naya Nah. I told you I'm off it. And you just gon call me dramatic so let's leave it alone.

Matcha No, I won't. (*Off* **Naya***'s look.*) I won't. Promise.

Naya . . . I just can't help. Feeling like. You're choosing death. Amongst other things.

Matcha O . . . kay. I ain't gon say you dramatic.

Naya Right, so—

Matcha But you are tripping.

Naya *wants to speak. Nods and smirks instead, daring* **Matcha** *to read her mind.*

Matcha What?

Naya Nothing. I. Nothing . . . I just. (*Small laugh.*) You . . . I just find it really funny how you really finessed me with that program shxt. I thought you had gone back to school all this. I mean, yes. Technically it is formal training. I won't invalidate that. I just think you have so much to offer and this is just. Damn.

Matcha Don't talk like that.

Naya It's my current thoughts. Maybe I'll feel different in a few hours or tomorrow, but presently I feel like you just lowered your life expectancy.

Matcha Baby, don't be dramaaatt—

She tries to swallow the word.

Fxck.

Naya Yup, I knew it was coming. Felt it before / your mouth opened.

Matcha Why does this mean that I'm seeking to die, though. You living in a foreign country for two years wasn't risky? Us being apart / for two years wasn't—

Naya Really, Matcha? I was in the Peace Corps. Peace. Corps. Not the Philadelphia Police Department. You can't possibly compare / the two.

Matcha What was that lil white lady's name that died in the name of peace? Ruthie, Rachel?

Naya You really trying it. For one, she wasn't in the Peace Corps.

Matcha Whatever. We are both working in service of others, of the people, right? How is that not comparable?

Naya   If they anything like the pigs in Michigan, they ain't too concerned / about the People.

Matcha   Wait. Naya, don't!

Naya   What?

Matcha   Could you maybe not? Just . . . don't.

Naya   What? First you beg me to tell you how I feel and / now you want me—

Matcha   Don't use that word. Please. It's dehumanizing as fxck.

Naya   Am I wrong though? . . . (*Adjusting*) Okay. I'm sorry, baby. I just. I guess I'm just overwhelmed.

I don't want to feel like I'm losing you right as I'm returning / to you.

Matcha   Whoa, whoa. Who said anything about losing me?

Naya   Um. History. Media. Common / fxckin sense.

Matcha   Can you please stop trying to kill me? It's just a job. A means to provide for you, me, and the little bad asses we gon raise together. I promise you: I got you.

Naya   . . . Okay. (*Off* **Matcha***'s look.*) Okay.

Matcha   You forreal this time?

Naya   I'm nervous. But I'm here for you, baby. You went for it. I mean you really / went for—

Matcha   I wanted to surprise you.

Naya   This is certainly a shocker, I'll tell you that.

Matcha   You really mad?

Naya   No. Matcha, look. I'm excited for you. I am. This is just . . . I mean, I ain't eem know Black folk was still signing up for the force.

Matcha   Come on, now.

Naya   Baby, I'm processing. You know joking's a part of my process.

Matcha   Yes. I do. I just think my need for your support and understanding blocked that particular memory.

Naya *opens her arms and* **Matcha** *melts into them.*

Matcha   I ever tell you that my dad was a cop.

Naya   I thought he was a gym teacher.

Matcha   He was. But only after he quit his cop job. Found out not long after I moved back here.

Naya   Wow.

Matcha   Yeah. That's what I said.

Naya   I didn't realize y'all were even allowed to quit. I thought it was blood in-blood out with the boys in blue. (*Off* **Matcha***'s look.*) Okay, I'm done. But wow, that's . . . [wild] about your dad . . . How long have you known th–doesn't matter . . . Is he why you decided to join?

Matcha   . . . No. Maybe one of them. Naya, look. Ever since I met you, I've wanted to do more. Not just say I do, but actually do it. I wanted to walk into rooms and have people know that whatever issue affected them and awaited me, I had at least two solutions in my back pocket. It may not be the most popular option, but it's one that I can live with for now. And I really hope you can too.

Naya   . . . Baby, I already said, "okay."

Matcha   I heard you. I want you to mean it. Need you to mean it.

A tea kettle whistles offstage.

Naya   The tea!

She hops up.

Matcha   Hawthorn?

Naya   Hibiscus. Hyssop. (*Slyly.*) Some of that high-grade Kush. Straight from the Volta region in Ghana. I snuck some back in a pair of rolled-up socks. Few other herbs. All infused to perfection. Wait . . . will you be able to drink it?

Matcha   Baby, I'm the law. There ain't nothing I can't do.

Naya   That's what I'm afraid of.

Section 4

Birth: Contemplating the Next Generation in a Complicated System

Impending motherhood has always been a joy tinged with terror for Black women. Since slavery in America the idea of not being able to protect one's offspring from harm is a fear that every Black woman has had to live with. As outlined in the first three sections of this book, America's systems can be a hostile welcome to new Black mothers. Be it the struggles to embrace Black beauty in a society that weaponizes the Black image, or the disparate inequality and access to resources in education, or the most feared, a policing system that targets black and brown bodies regardless of age, bringing Black children into the world has always come with a taxing emotional toll on Black parents. Add on top of these worries, the inequality in healthcare that creates a staggering statistic whereby Black women are at a higher risk of dying in childbirth than any other group of women in America. And yet, we push through these fears time and time again to usher our children into the world. In Dennis A. Allen II's *Within Untainted Wombs*, we see the dreams and fears of a Black woman who can communicate with her unborn child, illuminating the spectrum of emotions unique to Black expectant mothers. And in Deneen Reynolds-Knott's *Antepartum*, we see how shared experience and sisterhood help Black expectant mothers wade through these fears to advocate for themselves and their unborn children. Moreover, in both plays, we see Black women pushing through fear to push out their most prized possessions – a new Black life, a birth.

Foreword by Stacey Rose, The Fire This Time Festival Season 8 playwright, prolific writer for the stage and screen, and former respiratory specialist

Before I even dreamed of a life in the theater, I was a respiratory therapist. I started respiratory school in 1998 as a pregnant twenty-three-year-old who knew $7.10 an hour wasn't gonna cut it. My professors inferred and did what they could to ensure there was no way I was going to graduate the program on time, if at all. I had my son, Zion, the second semester of my first year. When he was just five days old, I received a call from one of my professors: "Be back in clinicals Monday or we're dropping you." Afraid for our future, I did what I needed to. I was in clinicals, stitches and all, the following Monday.

This experience foreshadowed the irreverence I witnessed Black women endure over the twenty-one years I spent in the field. From downplaying Black women's pain, to questioning whether their children "had the same daddy," to witnessing the postpartum death of a co-worker because no one would believe she couldn't breathe, my time in healthcare was often rough. I'm grateful for the times I, or other Black providers were there to intercede on their behalves. I hope that the lifting of these stories leads to substantive change in our medical practices. As my creative life expands, I will continue to shine light on these issues and the lives of all Black women. It's the way I'm still able to look out for them, and I'm so honored to do it.

Play #12: Within Untainted Wombs (an excerpt)
by Dennis A. Allen II

A Black woman is haunted by the voice of her unborn child.

Presented in The Fire This Time Festival Season 4, directed by Christopher Burris, performed by Lynette R. Freeman (**Mother**), W. Tre Davis (**Baby**), Lori E. Parquet (**Doctor**), and DeSean Stokes (**Shawn**).

Characters

Mother, *thirties, Black (African American).*
Shawn, *thirties, Black.*
Doctor, *Black female.*
Baby.

Time

Non-linear present.

Note

A breath: not to be taken literally—or maybe it is—inhale or exhale or both.
A moment: more of an emotional shift than a time indication—some moments take more time than others.
A minute: not to be taken literally—but can be—when paid attention to a minute always feels longer than it really is.

Within Untainted Wombs (an excerpt) *by Dennis A. Allen II*

Shawn (*off*)   No I don't have a damn appointment! Doctor?! Where is she?! Hey, doc!

Shawn *enters.*

Doctor   Excuse me, can I help you, sir?

Shawn   What the hell did you do to my wife?

Doctor   This is highly inappropriate, I'm ...

Shawn   What the hell did you do to my WIFE?!

Doctor   Who is ...

Shawn   My wife, Mother. You're the scientist that experimented on my wife, right?!

Doctor   I need you to calm down, Shawn? It's Shawn isn't it?

Shawn   What did you do?

Doctor   Is mother here?

Shawn   No, she's home in bed. Laid up in bed. Doctor's orders. Mandatory bed rest so not to risk losing the baby.

Doctor   What? Why didn't she call me? What happened?

Shawn   That's what I want to know. She was fine, completely fine until she came here.

Doctor   It was clearly detailed in the contract she signed that all gynecological concerns were to be handled by our staff.

Shawn   Gynecological concerns?

Doctor   We could be losing crucial data as we speak. You must take me to her.

Shawn   Crucial data? My wife and child's lives are in danger, doc.

Doctor   I will not have you speak to me in that tone.

Shawn   What are you the new age Marion Sims? You muthafuckas get off on playing God. You should know better! //

Doctor   You cannot walk in here and make blatantly misinformed speculative statements about me, about my work . . .

Shawn   // Smallpox in slaves, forty years of Tuskegee experiments with syphilis and shit, the Mississippi appendectomies, disguised hysterectomies performed on our Black women so that young doctors could gain experience performing the procedure.

Doctor   Nothing can be accomplished with you being paranoid and ignorantly accusatory, irrational behavior never . . .

Shawn   She told me you were Black. But I didn't believe. I didn't want to believe. You should know better!

Doctor   WHAT DO YOU WANT FROM ME?!

Shawn   Help her!

A moment.

Please. Help her.

A transition. **Shawn** *exits.* **Mother** *enters.*

Mother   Please I need your help.

Doctor   Mrs. Mckenzie, please have a seat.

Mother   I'm not sleeping and when I do . . . I dream about . . .

Doctor   Please. Please. Sit down. I've attempted to contact you since you stormed out of here. Would you like some water?

Mother   No. no thank you.

Doctor   Do you mind if I record us? The accuracy of your experience is.

Mother   That's fine. I'm quite comfortable with the camera these days actually.

Doctor   Really?

Recording begins. **Mother** *is projected on screen in real time.*

Mother   I convinced Shawn that we should make videos for the baby just in case, in case something happened to one of us, he'd at least have some sense of who we were.

Doctor   He?

Mother   It's a boy. A boy.

Doctor   What happened during your first connection?

Mother   You said there were others. FEMs?

Doctor   Yes.

Mother   Did they experience anything . . . strange?

Doctor   How do you mean?

Mother   When they talked with their babies did they say . . . what were the conversations like?

Doctor   I can't say specifically because that information could contaminate our study with you?

Mother   Contaminate?

Doctor   I mean to say, if you knew what the other mothers experienced it could influence how and what you communicate with your son hence . . .

Mother   Did their babies say anything crazy?

Doctor   Mrs. Mckenzie. What happened?

Mother   I had to tell Shawn I did this. I didn't want to, knew he wouldn't approve . . .

Screen flickers. **Doctor** *fades to background. Transition.* **Mother** *talks directly to camera.*

I'm recording these for you. I'm recording these just in case our family is cursed. How could you think I don't want you? That's wrong, it's wrong I want you! I want you. Do you know how happy your father will be when he finds out you're a boy?

Shawn *enters*

Shawn   Who's a boy?

Mother   Oh! You scared me!

Shawn   Who's a boy?

Shawn (*a breath*)   No? No?!

Wheewwwwww! What?! No?! I thought you wanted to wait?

Mother   I umm . . . .

Shawn (*silly chant dance song thingy*)

> Who put that stem on the apple. I did. I did.
> Who put that stem on the apple?
> I did. I did.

Mother   Shawn.

Shawn

> Who put that stem on the apple?! We did. We did.
> Come on girl dance with me.
> We did. We did. We did. We did.

Mother   I . . .

Shawn

> Come on, woman, I love . . .
> We did. We did.
> See there you go . . .
> We did. We did.

They dance a silly cheer-like dance together.

Mother *and* **Shawn**   We did.

Shawn   Who put that stem on the apple! What?!

Mother   We did. We did. We did. We did. We. did.

Shawn   Who put the . . . ah . . . baby?

Mother *starts to cry.*

Mother   I'm sorry. I'm okay.

Shawn   What I miss? Is this a hormonal moment?

Mother   Sorry. I'm fine. I'm fine.

Shawn   Yes. Yes you are.

He tenderly kisses **Mother.**

Shawn   So what changed your mind about knowing? You were afraid everyone would buy our baby yellow shit huh?

Mother   No. No.

Shawn I didn't realize you had an appointment today.

Mother I didn't.

Shawn Oh.

A minute.

Mother I enrolled in and participated in a clinical study that gave me the ability to see and speak to our unborn child. That's how I know he's a he because I met him today. And I know I should have talked to you about it first but I well I don't know why I didn't because I tell you everything and please don't be mad at me I just thought the money would be worth it and they promised no harm would come to me or the baby and the doctor was a woman, a Black woman at that, and how often do you get to meet a Black scientist that's a woman, I mean never I mean I never have and she seemed nice, a little cold, but nice and I promise never to do something like this without telling you again I just . . .

Shawn SHHHHHH . . .

Mother Shawn, baby, I'm sorry I . . .

Shawn I just need a minute. Okay? Okay.

He exits. Screen flickers. **Doctor** *reemerges.*

Doctor What did your husband do, Mrs. Mckenzie?

Mother Do? He didn't "do" anything. When he gets overwhelmed emotionally he puts himself in isolation. Secludes himself until he's sure he can deal in a calm and logical manner. He processes it and moves on. I've always been jealous of how he can just move on.

Doctor Hm. You mentioned irregular sleep patterns.

Mother No. I said I'm not sleeping.

Doctor Why are you not sleeping Mrs. Mckenzie?

(A breath.) Mrs. Mckenzie?

Mother Hook me back up.

Doctor I'm sorry?

Mother To the machine. Hook me back up.

Doctor I'd much rather finish the report from your first experience, protocol requires that I . . .

Mother Doctor, if you want me to share with you my "experience" I suggest you hook me up. Now!

(A moment.) **Doctor** *gets the device and a pill.*

Doctor Okay same as before, take this pill, I'm going to be here to monitor your vitals.

Mother *puts on the device. A moment. The screen flickers then a montage of news footage and pictures of the Scottsboro boys, Central Park Five, Rodney King, Rubin*

Hurricane Carter, Trayvon Martin, Emmett Till, Death of Dr. Martin Luther King Jr., Malcolm X, Medgar Evers, Sean Bell, gang-related murders, lynching images . . . etc. . . . the montage cycle increase in speed during **Baby** *and* **Mother**'s *interaction.* **Baby** *enters.*

Mother   This is not all that there is to life. There's so much more, so much more.

Doctor   Your heart rate has increased substantially. Can you repeat what he's saying? What you see?

Baby   I don't want to be born.

Mother   A Black man is president of the United States, you'll be born into a world where that's a reality, to a generation that won't know any different.

Baby   It hurts!

I don't want to be born.

Mother   I'm afraid, yes I'm afraid. I admit it. Everything about your birth scares the shit out of me. That it could kill me. That I have no idea, no basic blueprint on how to raise you or how to be a good mother. Yes. That Shawn will find me fat and unattractive and eventually leave me because you represent an actual loss of freedom for him. For us. But mostly I'm afraid that . . . that . . .

Baby   Man's best friend is only that, when he clearly belongs to Man.

Mother   It will be better. It will be better while you're growing up.

Baby   You don't believe that.

Mother   You are loved. You will be loved. By both of us in a stable household. Do you know how rare that is, how special that is? I want you. We want you. Baby I know you can feel my love. I know you can.

Baby   Hurts.

Mother   You have to trust me when I say . . .

She wheezes, struggling to catch her breath.

You have to trust me when I say . . .

Doctor   Mrs. Mckenzie? What's wrong? Mrs. Mckenzie?

Baby   I don't want to be born.

Screen flickers then resumes live action feed. **Baby** *exits.* **Doctor** *takes glasses off of* **Mother**. **Mother** *continues to struggle for breath.*

Doctor   You didn't indicate that you had asthma in your chart.

Mother   I . . . I . . . I . . .

Doctor   Okay just focus on breathing. Do you have a pump in your purse? Mrs. Mckenzie?

Doctor   Mrs. Mckenzie!

Mother *loses consciousness.*

Play #13: Antepartum *by Deneen Reynolds-Knott*

Two pregnant women navigate bedrest and broken expectations in a hospital's antepartum unit.

Presented in The Fire This Time Festival Season 11, directed by Ebony Noelle Golden, performed by Antu Yacob (**Autumn**), Paris Cymone (**Mara**), and Cary Hite (**Meal Service Assistant/Dr. Niles**).

Characters

Autumn, *Black woman, late thirties, pregnant.*
Mara, *Black woman, early thirties, pregnant.*
Meal Service Assistant/Dr. Niles, *played by same actor, Black man, forty.*

Time and Place

The present. The antepartum unit of a large university hospital.

Antepartum: A Ten-Minute Play *by Deneen Reynolds-Knott*

Lights up on:

Hospital room. A window. Two beds. Side tables on wheels next to each bed. A curtain drawn between them.

Mara *sleeps in the bed closest to the window.* **Autumn** *sits up in the bed on the other side of the curtain.*

A **Meal Service Assistant** *enters and places a tray with a covered plate, bowl, and juice plus three menus on* **Mara**'*s table.* **Mara** *stirs. The* **Assistant** *exits and re-enters placing a similar tray on* **Autumn**'*s table. The* **Assistant** *exits.*

Mara *wakes. She sees the drawn curtain.*

Mara   Hello?

Autumn   Hi?

Mara   I didn't hear them bring anyone in. How long have you been here?

She sits up.

Autumn   I don't know. It was late. Or really early.

Mara *brings her breakfast closer to her. She uncovers her food.*

Mara   If you wanna pull back the curtain. It's fine. I know it can get dark over there. It's a nice view. I have no problem sharing it.

Autumn   Oh. Okay. Thanks.

Mara   You can open it now or—

Autumn   I don't think I can reach it, though.

She tries to reach the curtain. **Mara** *does and opens it. They look at one another.* **Mara** *smiles.*

Mara   Hi. I'm Mara.

Autumn   Hi. Autumn.

Mara (*re: the view*)   The park's really in bloom now.

They look out the window.

Autumn   How long have you been here?

Mara   Uh. A month on Friday. (*Caresses her belly.*) She's staying put.

She eats a little. **Autumn** *uncovers her food.*

Mara   You didn't get to choose your breakfast. They always give the worst stuff when you don't.

Looks at **Autumn**'s *plate.*

Yeah. That's what they did.

Picks up bagged muffin from tray.

This muffin isn't bad. Want it?

Autumn   I'm okay.

She picks a little at her tray. **Mara** *looks through her menus.*

Mara   Make sure to fill out the menus. For lunch, the cream of broccoli soup is really good. Dinner? The chicken parmigiana is much better than it should be. Never get the rice pilaf. It's always under-cooked.

She circles her choices with a pen. **Autumn** *follows.*

Autumn   How are the Swedish meatballs?

Mara *looks at* **Autumn** *and shakes her head solemnly.*

Mara   But the chocolate pudding is delicious.

Autumn   How many weeks are you?

Mara   Thirty-three.

Autumn   So when you got here—

Mara   My water broke week 29. Just a couple of days shy of thirty.

(*Beat.*) How many weeks are you?

Autumn Twenty-six.

(*Beat.*) That's bad. Isn't it?

Mara Just tell the little one to relax and stay put. We're making it to term.

(*Smiles. Beat.*) Have any of those NICU doctors talked to you yet?

Autumn No.

Mara Then they're coming. All nice with their, "Hey. We want to tell you about the NICU to prepare you for what happens after your baby is born and answer any concerns or questions." Make sure they take your insurance, cause I talked to one of those jokers for ten minutes when I was admitted. They charged me 600 dollars and my insurance won't cover it.

Autumn 600 dollars? For ten minutes?

Mara Mmm. Hmm.

Autumn Why didn't I become a doctor?

Mara I'm sayin'.

Beat.

Did you go on one of the maternity tours here?

Autumn No.

Mara They don't talk about this antepartum unit on the tour. Guess they're not trying to scare a bunch of expecting people.

Autumn We were still deciding between a home birth or the birthing center. Had a whole plan in my head.

Mara What was the plan?

Autumn (*hesitates*) Doesn't matter now. You were planning on delivering here?

Mara (*nods*) Yeah. I have fibroids, so. Something about where they're located. Don't think I would've been cleared for a birthing center.

Autumn This your first child?

Mara No. I have a three-year-old. She's actually mad at me for being here. She won't talk to me, when my husband brings her.

Autumn She misses you.

Mara Your first?

Autumn Yes. Was your daughter early too?

Mara No. It's a mystery.

Autumn (*sighs*) Last night, I was eating dinner at home. It was a hot day, so I had on this linen skirt and suddenly the back of it was drenched. Now I'm in this bed. And the best case scenario is that I'll be lying here for a very long time. So weird.

Mara   I was teaching. Standing at the whiteboard writing and I could feel the trickle. It was warm. Felt so strange and wrong. But I kept writing and kept talking. Class ended. Still took questions from students after class. Standing there. Leaking. Reassuring Charles about his grade. Then I came straight here.

Beat.

They come by and change our padding. But if yours gets too wet, there's extra in that table.

Autumn   Oh. Okay.

Mara   Some days it's a really slow leak and some days it's a lot. But that's just me.

Dr. Niles *enters.*

Dr. Niles   Good morning. (*Noticing curtain is open.*) Oh, so this is the social room. Hello.

Mara   Hello.

Autumn   Good morning.

Dr. Niles   Hello, Ms. Williams. I'm Dr. Niles from the neo-natal intensive care unit, where your baby will be admitted. I wanted to take a few moments to tell you about the unit and our process. Also, answer any questions you have.

Autumn *looks at* **Mara** *and back at* **Dr. Niles**.

Autumn   What insurance do you take?

Dr. Niles   Oh. That's a very smart question.

Autumn   Well.

Dr. Niles   What insurance do you have?

Autumn   Blue Cross.

Dr. Niles   I do not accept Blue Cross.

Autumn   I can't talk to you. Do any of the other doctors in there take Blue Cross?

Dr. Niles   I don't think so, but I'll ask around.

Mara   For free? She's refusing this service.

Autumn   Yes. This is a refusal. Go away.

Beat.

That was way more emphatic than I meant it.

Dr. Niles   I understand.

Autumn   You seem like a nice person.

Dr. Niles   Thanks? I'll go.

Autumn   Yes. Bye.

Dr. Niles   Have a good day.

He exits.

Mara (*calling after him*)   Don't charge her!

Autumn   Wait. So it's possible that none of those NICU doctors take our insurance? But our babies will be in there. What does that mean?

Mara   It means . . . so many bills I'm never opening.

Beat.

He never said he wouldn't charge you. You notice that?

Autumn   You think he will?

Mara *shrugs.*

Autumn (*re: cell phone on side table*)   I should have recorded that conversation.

Mara   Record me. I'm a witness. I look a mess, but I can vouch for you.

Autumn   You sure?

Mara   Yeah.

Autumn *gets her cell phone and points the phone's camera at* **Mara***.* **Mara** *fusses with her hair for a sec.*

Autumn   Recording.

Mara (*for the camera*)   Hello. I'm Mara Price. It's Tuesday. Right?

Autumn *nods.*

Mara   Tuesday. June . . .

Autumn (*for the camera*)   23rd.

Mara (*for the camera*)   Yes. It's Tuesday, June 23rd. You lose track of time in here. I'm with Autumn. Williams?

Autumn (*shooting*)   Mmm-hmm.

Mara (*for the camera*)   Autumn Williams just refused a conversation with Dr. Niles from the NICU. He didn't give her any information and she should not be billed because no service was rendered. (*To* **Autumn**.) Okay.

Autumn (*stops recording*)   Thanks.

Mara (*laughs*)   I don't think that would be admissible anywhere.

Autumn   How many roommates have you had?

Mara   You're the fourth.

Autumn   Did any of them make it to thirty-seven weeks?

Mara *shakes her head.* **Autumn** *touches her belly and gets lost in a sad thought.*

Mara (*reassuring*)   They were pre-term, but I hear the babies are okay.

Beat.

We get to hear their heartbeats every day. They'll probably take you in before lunch. Do you know if you're having a girl or boy?

Autumn   I'm not supposed to, but one of the nurses let it slip. I'm trying to forget what I heard.

Mara   Sorry.

Just one more thing, right?

Autumn *shrugs.*

Beat.

Autumn   I wanted only natural light and candles. The whole room would've smelled like lavender.

Mara   I love lavender.

Autumn   I squat on a birthing ball. I'm breathing deeply. My partner massages my legs with peppermint oil. I sip a smoothie made of honeydew and kiwi.

Mara   Mmmm.

Autumn   And there's soothing music playing.

Mara   What music?

Autumn   Solange.

Mara   Yes.

Autumn   And I hold our baby, welcoming them to the world. We take a warm bath together with healing herbs. I kiss their soft skin. And we snuggle.

Mara   That's really beautiful.

Autumn *slumps with grief.*

Mara   We can close this, if you need. (*Re: the curtain, compassionately.*)

Autumn   Could we?

Mara   Sure. Just let me know if you want it open again. It's no problem at all.

She closes the curtain between them. **Autumn** *lies down.* **Mara** *opens the bagged muffin and eats. Beat.*

Autumn   Good looking out, Mara.

Mara   Anytime.

Autumn *lies.* **Mara** *eats.*

Lights dim.

Section 5

Maintaining Roots: Addressing Gentrification in Historically Black Neighborhoods

Over the past decade New York City has seen rapid gentrification in historically Black neighborhoods. This sudden influx of wealthier and primarily white residents to these areas has not only threatened to displace multiple generations of Black families, but the communities and local customs that grew in these areas. The effects of rapid gentrification in these neighborhoods has not only been a much discussed hot button topic in various local governments over the years, it has been explored on stages large and small, and The Fire This Time plays have been no exception. Bernard Tarver's *Another Sunday in the Park* and Cyrus Aaron's *Panopticon* delve into the myriad ways that white gentrification in Black neighborhoods, and a lack of sensitivity to the locals who have been there for years, can have detrimental consequences for all seeking to live peacefully.

Foreword by Michelle Tyrene Johnson, The Fire This Time Festival Season 11 playwright, award-winning author, playwright, and journalist who covers race, culture, and identity

Since March 2020, my life has featured an atypical amount of moving—starting with selling the family home. The house was in poor condition, but there was still sadness in letting my grandparents' house go. Homes and neighborhoods can be physical manifestations of the heart. That attachment is particularly strong in the Black community where there is emotional safety in numbers.

The plays of Cyrus Aaron and Bernard Tarver hit on this—how culture and the truest sense of "homecoming" can be seemingly obliterated in the blink of a chugged down kombucha. We see how easily our community rituals can be "othered" by a white woman who believes the police are her personal secret service detail. With Aaron's Panopticon *I laughed hard. I'm a girl from the hood whose bougie tastes exceed my public radio/playwriting income. Gentrification is like bringing another language to the neighborhood. And I'm embarrassingly bilingual.*

But I'm Black, Black, Blackety Black, all day, everyday Black. So in Tarver's Just Another Sunday in the Park *my blood instinctively boiled at even a fictional Karen trying to police a Black neighborhood as a gentrifying interloper. As a playwright, I often write a concocted brew of Afro-futurism intertwined with historical reimagining. I believe the truest love story of the human condition is Black authenticity.*

The crime of gentrification isn't that white money snuffs out Black culture. That can't happen. Rather, it's the high cost of having to constantly re-plant our roots. Which we do.

Play #14: Just Another Saturday in the Park
by Bernard Tarver

When two people meet in the park one morning, the past, present, and future of their neighborhood collide.

Presented in The Fire This Time Season 10, directed by Kevin R. Free, performed by Cherrye J. Davis (**Sarita Cash**), Dana Costello (**Heather Stall**), and Carl Fisk (**Officer Bryan Touhey**).

Characters

Sarita Cash,* *Black female, mid/late thirties, a member of the African Ancestral Drum Circle, a collective of Black women who meet every Saturday morning in Jackson Park to drum. She owns a home a block away.*
Heather Stall, *white female, mid/late thirties, a new homeowner in the neighborhood and vice president of the newly formed Jackson Park Neighborhood Improvement Association.*
Officer Brian Touhey, *White male, mid/late twenties, a police officer.*

*Actor will need some ability to play a djembe.

Setting

A park in a mid-size American city.

Time

Very much in the present.

Just Another Saturday in the Park: A Ten-Minute Play *by Bernard J. Tarver*

With lights up one-third, we see **Sarita Cash**, *a Black woman in her mid/late thirties, seated on a small stool near a tree, playing a djembe. It's a summer morning, outdoors in Jackson Park. Eyes closed, animated in her movements, she plays as if directly inspired by the ancestors. Perhaps she is playing for them? She is so into her music she has tuned out everything and everyone around her.*

She continues to play as lights rise to full. **Heather Stall**, *a white female in her mid/late thirties, enters, talking on a cellphone. As she observes from a distance, she finishes up her conversation and puts the phone away. She waits before approaching.*

Then **Sarita** *hits one final note on the djembe, settles into herself and reconnects with her surroundings.* **Heather** *sees her opening.*

Heather   Excuse me. (*Beat.*) Hello!

Sarita (*startled*)   Oh! (*Beat.*) Sorry, I didn't see you standing there. You startled me.

Heather   I didn't mean to frighten you.

Sarita   No, my bad. I was kinda in my own world.

Heather   I can see that.

Sarita   Yeah, drumming does that to me. When I'm feeling it, when I'm really into a rhythm, it's like a spiritual awakening. I'm in a whole other world.

Heather   Fascinating . . .

Sarita   Sometimes I could just play for hours.

Heather   Well, now we wouldn't want that, would we!

Sarita   I don't mean it literally.

Heather (*relieved*)   Thank God.

Sarita   Huh?

Heather   Are you done now with the drumming? (*Beat.*) You and your friends? You seem to go on so long!

Sarita   We only play for about an hour . . .

Heather   We've noticed. It seems so long. (*Beat.*) Bright and early, every Saturday morning . . . /

Sarita (*sensing something*)   / . . . But we're done by 9:00, 9:30 at the latest.

Heather   Well, it's not when you finish that's the issue.

Sarita *rises from her seat, startling* **Heather** *who takes a step back.*

Sarita   Issue? What issue? (*Beat.*) And, who are you again?

Heather   I'm sorry. I didn't introduce myself. Where are my manners?

Sarita   I don't know.

Heather   I'm Heather Stall. I live in the neighborhood. I've been asked to talk to you, or someone in your group, about the drumming.

Sarita (*sarcastically*)   Do you want to join us? Everyone is welcome. Just bring your own drum.

Heather   No, no. That's not what I mean. I think you know that.

Sarita   Well, what do you mean?

Heather   This early morning drumming has just got to stop! You're disturbing the peace.

Sarita   Disturbing the peace? Am I under arrest? Are you a police officer, Heather Stall?

Heather   No.

Sarita   Well, then where do you get off telling me we have to stop?

Heather   We have a right to peace and quiet on a Saturday morning. We've paid an awful lot to live in this neighborhood and we shouldn't have to put up with all this noise.

Sarita   Who is this *we* you're referring to? *We've* been playing in this park every Saturday morning for the past six years. This is the first time I've ever laid eyes on you. Who the hell are you trying to speak for the whole neighborhood?

Heather   I don't think I like your tone. For your information, I'm the vice president of the Jackson Park Neighborhood Improvement Association.

Sarita   The Jackson Park what?

Heather   Neighborhood Improvement Association . . ./

Sarita   /. . . I heard you the first time.

Heather   We formed the association two months ago because we were concerned about conditions in the area, the noise in the park being one of them.

Sarita   Noise? (*Trying to remain composed.*) See, I'm just gonna ignore that comment for now because I'm trying to figure out how you formed a neighborhood association without inviting any of the people who already live here.

Heather (*defensive*)   We paid a lot of money for our homes, and even more in property taxes. I think we have a right to say who gets to gather in our park.

Sarita   Your park? How long have you been living here?

Heather (*proudly*)   My husband and I bought that house over there last September, if you must know. (*Pointing off stage.*)

Sarita   And they already made you vice president of the association? You go, Heather! (*Beat.*) Now, you see that house over there (*Pointing off stage.*), the pretty green one with the garden in front? That's my house. I live here too. My wife and I bought it nine years ago! (*Beat.*) You ain't even been here a whole year, talking about *your* park!

Heather (*defensive*)   I don't think it matters how long someone lives here in order to see what needs fixing.

Sarita   It matters that you formed a group and excluded the people who were living here before you. You fix that, then we can talk about what the real issues are. Now kindly get the hell out of my face, Heather Stall.

Sarita *starts to gather up her things, when* **Officer Brian Touhey**, *a white male police officer in his mid/late twenties, enters.* **Heather** *notices him first.*

Heather   Over here, officer!

Sarita   Oh, no you didn't!

Officer Touhey   Somebody call about a noise complaint?

Heather   Yes, officer. I did. I called you a half hour ago.

Officer Touhey   What's the problem?

Heather   Officer, my name is Heather Stall. I'm vice president of the Jackson Park Neighborhood Improvement Association. We're a group of concerned homeowners trying to clean up the neighborhood. We want to improve conditions in and around the park for families trying to safely raise children here.

Officer Touhey *maintains a professional neutrality. He takes out his memo book to write down notes.*

Officer Touhey   So what's the problem?

Heather   My husband and I bought the home right over there (*Pointing*). We love the park. It's so convenient. He likes to jog. I come here to sit and read or just enjoy nature, but I suppose there's always a downside. (*Beat.*) This woman here and her friends . . . they get together practically at the crack of dawn every single week and start a God-awful racket on those bongos.

Sarita   Bongos? Are you for real? Look . . . if you're gonna make up shit at least get it right! It's a djembe!

Officer Touhey (*to* **Sarita**)   Ma'am, please. I'll get your side of the story in a moment.

Sarita (*under her breath*)   Bongos . . .

Heather   I don't know what you call them but they sure make a lot of noise. We all hear it and we don't think we should have to put up with it, don't you agree? We need you to make them stop the noise and stop hanging out in the park.

Officer Touhey   Ma'am, I'm not sure what I can do, but let me talk to the lady here.

Heather   Thank you, officer. Hopefully you can set them straight so that we don't have to resort to other means.

Officer Touhey *crosses to* **Sarita**, *while* **Heather** *casts a confident gaze in her direction.*

Officer Touhey   May I have you name please?

Sarita   My name is Sarita Cash. I own that house over there (*Pointing.*) and lived here for the past nine years.

Officer Touhey   The lady claims your drum playing was making a lot of noise?

Sarita   It's called a djembe.

Officer Touhey   Your *djembe* . . . she says it was disturbing her.

Sarita   Officer, there's a group of us. We're the African Ancestral Drum Circle. Most of us live in the neighborhood. We've been gathering in the park every Saturday morning for the past six years. No one has ever complained, until today. You can look it up. We do other cultural programs too . . . in the park . . . at the public library . . . for Black History Month, Juneteenth, Kwanzaa, the Food Festival, you name it. (*Beat.*) Didn't I see you working security at the Food Festival last year?

Officer Touhey   Maybe. I worked that day.

Sarita   Then you've probably heard us. (*Beat.*) Our drumming is an expression of our history and culture, which we share with anyone in the community who is interested. (*Beat.*) I don't know what noise she's talking about. We don't make noise. We drum for a purpose.

She returns **Heather***'s gaze.* **Officer Touhey** *suddenly realizes what he's in the middle of.*

Officer Touhey   Ladies, without first-hand observation, I'm not really in a position to determine whether or not this is a legitimate noise complaint . . . /

Heather   / . . . But I just told you it was.

Officer Touhey   But I didn't hear anything myself and without that, it's just she said/she said.

Heather   So you're not going to do anything. Not even issue a ticket?

Officer Touhey   Ma'am, my hands are tied. I haven't seen or heard anything.

Heather   But don't you have to have some sort of permit to gather and perform in the park?

Sarita   We're not selling tickets.

Officer Touhey   The park is open from 7:00 am to 11:00 pm every day, and anyone is free to use it.

Heather   So I guess we'll just have to keep calling the police every Saturday, and hope you move fast enough to get here to hear it for yourselves.

Sarita   That would be making nuisance calls. You could get arrested for that.

Officer Touhey   Ma'am, you can do as you wish. If we come and we hear anything that appears to create a disturbance of the peace, we'll address it then. But right now, there's nothing I can do.

Heather   Our property taxes pay for the upkeep of this park, you know. They pay your salary too. Thank you, officer. You've been of no help today.

Officer Touhey   If there's nothing else, I'll be on my way.

He turns to leave.

Heather   Officer, I want your name and badge number.

Officer Touhey   Excuse me?

Heather   I'll need it for my report, in case my association wants to take further legal action. Our president is very close with the mayor, you know.

Officer Touhey   No, I didn't know. (*Beat.*) Officer Brian Touhey. Badge number 3-6-8-7-3. Shall I spell the last name?

Heather   No need. But don't be surprised if you hear from me again.

Officer Touhey   I'm sure I won't. (*Beat.*) Good day, ladies.

He exits. As **Heather** *stews,* **Sarita** *tries to contain her amusement. The awkward silence is palpable.*

Heather   I hope you don't think this is the end.

Sarita   What is your problem? You just moved here and right away want to start telling everybody else what to do. Who does that?

Heather   We have a right to peace and quiet.

Sarita   And we have a right to drum in the park!

Heather   You don't own this park.

Sarita   And neither do you! I'm not trying to!

Heather   People want to enjoy it without being surrounded by noise and sketchy strangers.

Sarita (*to herself*)   Hooo! Breathe, Sarita. Breathe. (*Beat.*) You know, I came here today to enjoy myself. The sun is shining. It's not too hot. I got to drum with my friends. I'm having a good day! But you? You need to chill the fuck out.

Heather   See, and your tone is so rude and disrespectful. Your profanity is so unnecessary.

Sarita   But not unprovoked. (*Beat.*) Your little police call didn't work out the way you wanted. So you can move on now.

Heather   I'll be watching you people . . . and listening.

Sarita   Leave, before I take my cellphone camera out and make you go viral.

Pissed but determined to fight another day, **Heather** *exits.*

Sarita *feels somewhat drained by the whole experience and sits on her stool. She alternately tries to compose herself and cleanse the area of negative energy. Once she has regained her equilibrium, she takes her djembe and begins to play. Softly at first, then with more intensity as . . .*

Lights fade.

Play #15: Panopticon *by Cyrus Aaron*

Things are heating up outside, and two middle-aged men take a familiar spot in their neighborhood and shoot the breeze. They must face the fact that everything around them is changing drastically, but the one thing they intend to keep is their perspective.

Presented in The Fire This Time Season 11, directed by Ebony Noelle Golden, performed by James Edward Becton (**Curtis**), Cary Hite (**Hill**), and Paris Cymone (**Tonya**).

Characters

Curtis, *a sixty-something Black man born and bred in the neighborhood.*
Hill, *a younger-sixty-something Black man born and bred in the neighborhood.*
Tonya, *a Black woman in her late twenties; a transplant from the Midwest.*

Time

Late Spring, May 2019.

Setting

The corner of Hancock and Tompkins in Bedford-Stuyvesant, Brooklyn, New York.

Panopticon *by Cyrus Aaron*

Scene One

It's early Friday morning, and it's already 80 degrees. Winter hangs around like a stubborn ex, but warm weather is moving in with plans to stay. Two men in their sixties arrange chairs on the edge of the newly rehabbed Healthy Choice Market—formerly known as Deli Corp Bodega. One of the men enters Healthy Choice. The former bodega flosses a pristine green sign that holds white lettering, with colorful images of fruits, and just below, floor-to-ceiling glass with automatic sliding doors at the center. Between the entrance and where the men have placed their chairs is a bright red bench for customers. The storefront looks like it was placed on the street, like a new hotel property on a worn Monopoly board. A few feet away, a metal trash can is overflowing with Styrofoam containers, bottles, and plastic bags—it stands immoveable and sacred, a low-income shrine.

Curtis *exits the bodega, but stops, amazed and disgusted by the sliding doors.*

Curtis   I need a got damn drink; can't believe this jive muthafucka.

Hill   I told you not to waste your time. I tried to tell ya.

Curtis   This nigga Emir ain't got no quarter-bag chips.

Hill   Chips ain't been a quarter for a long time, Curt.

Curtis   That ain't the point. A quarter, two quarters, it don't matter, he don't sell 'em. Instead, this nigga got the audacity to try and sell me some damn . . . what he call 'em . . . "KETTLE BRAND CHIPS," fa fo' damn dollas. Talkin' bout it's "Himalayan Sea Salt and Vinegar." Nigga, all I want is some basic ass no-name-salt and vinegar chips for 50 cents.

Hill   Those days are over. You knew that when Emir closed for renovations. If you want "Utz," you gone have to take your ass down to Fulton.

Curtis   But Hill . . . what street is this?

Hill   Hancock.

Curtis   And what street we live on?

Hill   Man, you know where the hell you live.

Curtis *just stares at* **Hill**.

Hill   Is this dementia? . . . How many fingers I got up? Do you even know what street we live on?

Curtis *stares even harder.*

Hill   . . . It's just stupid that I got to answer some shit you already know the answer to . . . and you not gone stop looking at me until I say it, huh?. . . Hancock, you live on Hancock, Curt.

Curtis   Exactly. So, what I look like, walking five blocks to Fulton because I got a taste for some damn chips! The whole point of a bodega is to be conveniently located on your corner and sell you the shit that you like.

A passerby walks into the store sounding off the door sensor.

Curtis *throws his hands in the air at the sound of the doors.*

The muthafucka got sliding doors!

Hill   I know one thing; that doorbell gon' get on my last nerve. We got to hear that every time somebody walk in and out?

The same passerby exits the store.

Curtis   Every time, Hill.

He dramatically takes a seat. **Hill** *hands him a brown paper bag, and* **Curtis** *takes a swig.*

Curtis   He done forgot where he come from. That's all it is. Forgot he a nigga just like us.

Hill   Emir ain't never been no nigga. He own too much property to be a nigga. Brown on the outside, but white on the inside.

Curtis   Man get the hell outta here with that. We own too.

Hill   Nigga you ain't never owned a thing in your life.

Curtis   I wasn't talking about me.

Hill   Well, you said "We."

Curtis   Nig . . . You know what I meant. We as a community . . . These blocks used to be ours. Joe Hightower's laundromat was the longest-running business WE had.

Hill   And THEY moved HIS black ass outta here. Ain't no sign of Joe or the laundromat. All WE got is what THEY build—like that big ass piece of shit across the street.

He motions to the new large development that stretches the entire block and towers over everything else.

Curtis   Whatever the fuck THAT is.

Hill   Don't know what it's s'posed to be, but it ain't what it used to be.

Curtis   Shit just big for no reason.

Hill   Blocking the sun too.

Curtis   Ain't that somethin'? A glass building the size of the whole block blocks the sun . . . and you can't see shit inside.

Hill   You think they watching us?

Curtis   Probably . . .

Hill *and* **Curtis** *stick out their middle fingers at the building and throw in a crouch grab for an extra emphasis. Their antics make them erupt in laughter.*

Hill   Listen . . . I bet you they hold KKK meetings, probably hiding Donald Trump's ass in there.

Curtis   Hill, you crazy. You know that Hi-C orange piece of shit won't be caught dead in the Stuy . . . unless he wanna get caught dead in the Stuy, you hear me?

Hill   I got some reparations for that ass.

Hill *and* **Curtis** *continue laughing, dapping and shaking up in agreement.*

Curtis   You know what? I think you on to somethin'. All these beanie-hat-flip-flop wearing hipsters moving in here . . . they probably host some kind of sensitivity training shit for the liberal whites.

Hill   Like a gentrifiers anonymous?

Curtis   GENTRIFIERS ANONYMOUS!

He roleplays by slapping **Hill** *with his white-girl ponytail.*

Curtis (*white fragility tears*)   Hi, my name is Rachel . . .

Hill   Hi, Rachel.

Curtis   . . . And I'm . . . a gentrifier.

Hill *consoles* **Curtis**.

Hill   There, there, you detached and delusional white girl . . . Rachel, will you join me in prayer?

Both   Lord, grant me the serenity to accept the things I cannot change, the courage to change the things I can, and the wisdom to know the difference.

Laughter erupts again between them.

Curtis   You's a silly muthafucka, Hill.

Hill   But you see what I'm saying though . . . As big as that building is, it ain't got no signage. That ain;t nothing but a trap house for white people.

Curtis   Oooooouuu. That's some scary shit when you think about it . . . White folks slang the shit out of hate . . .

Hill   Keep it a buck with you. I think that building is a racist.

Curtis   Now hold on now, Hill; how can a building be a racist?

Hill   Institutionalized racism, my brother. The same way these brownstones have good bones, these developers putting racist bones inside these new buildings. It ain't about family and community no more, especially not the Black family. Man, it's about money and greed. And when it becomes about the all-mighty dollar you can make any amount of square footage serve your kind of evil . . . We don't belong. That's how I feel when I walk into banks, courthouses . . . shit I even felt like that at my job, and they hired me.

Curtis   Like that new spot on Jefferson. I didn't feel comfortable sitting at the bar, and you know I never met a bar that didn't like my black ass.

Hill   They stopped making physical white-only signs a long time ago, but we still know what's for us and what ain't. It's in the rent, it's in the doorman, it's even in the kind of chips they sell you.

Curtis *picks up the brown paper bag and sips.*

Curtis   Preach . . . I ain't look at it that way until you said it. You got a point . . . cause the other day . . .

Hill   Of course, I gotta point. I ain't talking out my ass, nigga.

Curtis   I know, man, I said . . . I'm trying to agree with your ass by telling you a story . . . JUST LISTEN. Now the other day . . . I'm sitting in the car double parked, and this little white girl opens my door and gets in the backseat.

Hill   You lyin'?

Curtis   Do you know this dumb broad thought I was an Uber driver? Had the nerve to come at me sideways cause I ain't pull off when she got in, talkin' bout she in a rush.

Hill (*laughs*)   You know, white folks don't ever see shit right. You can be twelve and they'll swear up and down you twenty-two. In your apartment and swear it's they crib. All they know about Black is what they want to use it for.

Curtis   They not kicking us off this corner, Hill. Fuck that. We been here before this street even had a name.

Hill   First off, don't try to age me, nigga, our folks was driving Buicks not horses and buggies.

Curtis   You know what I mean.

Hill   I get what you sayin' but who gone stop 'em, Curt? It ain't gone be us. You gone sit your old ass down, sip this cognac, and hope these young niggas do something different.

He sees someone in the distance and begins fixing himself and organizing the table.

Hold that thought, nigga. (*Clears throat.*)

Tonya *walks up on the men. She is casually dressed wearing a shirt with a picture of a young Angela Davis and carries a tote bag with the words "Buy Weed from Women."*

Tonya   Hey, Mr. Curtis.

Curtis   Hey there, Ms. Tonya!

Tonya *looks at* **Hill** *with less enthusiasm.*

Tonya   Sir.

Hill   Tonya, why you only call Curtis "Mister"? I know I look handsomely younger, but old Curt and I bout the same age.

Tonya   Because Mr. Curtis acts his age.

Hill   What you trying to say; I'm not age appropriate?

Tonya   Hill, in the two years I've lived here, I ain't found nothing appropriate about you.

Hill (*shocked*)   But, Tonya. *Mi cheri amor*, I greet you with such love.

Tonya   That ain't love you greeting me with, Hill.

Hill   What? I carry a compliment just for you. Can't count how many times I've called you beautiful. I always tell you when you looking sexy as hell . . . if it was up to me, you'd be on every billboard in Times Square . . .

Tonya   Hill, I am not your pin-up girl. Are you finished?

Hill   You want me to keep going? Cause you know I can.

Tonya   You're right, Hill. Your words are compliments.

Hill *gets excited and pops* **Curtis** *in the arm.*

Tonya   However, I can read your old, nasty mind, and your body language ain't complimenting me, it's harassing me.

Curtis   Teach this old dog, Tonya.

Hill   Shut your old ass up, Hill. I ain't harassed nobody.

Tonya   Anyway. Mr. Curtis, y'all drinking already? The bank not even open yet.

Hill   Yeah, but the doors of the church are always open. Amen?

Tonya   Something is really wrong with you.

Curtis   I know it's early, Tonya, but we had to.

Tonya   Had to?

Curtis   Everything is changing, Tonya.

Hill   And nobody asked us for our input!

Tonya   And what's your input?

Hill   We want these young niggas . . .

Curtis *gives* **Hill** *a look.*

Hill   We would like for the men of your generation to do what we couldn't and take back the neighborhood. Before everything turns into glass and shatters into nothing.

Tonya   What are you expecting the younger generation to do that you can't do for yourself?

Another passerby enters the bodega, and all three react to the bell.

Tonya   Ooohhhhh. I see. So, I take it you don't like the changes Emir made to the bodega?

Curtis   Ms. Tonya, it has automatic sliding doors.

Tonya   Well, did you consider it's now wheelchair accessible . . .

Curtis *opens his mouth to respond, but realizes he overlooked the ramp.*

Hill (*laughing*)   She got your ass with that one.

Curtis   Negro, hush. You ain't ever seen nobody roll in no damn bodega for a bacon, egg, and cheese.

Tonya   Probably because it wasn't accessible.

Hill   She got you again. I mean how you know Miss Glenda over on Macon ain't been dying to slide through for a bacon, egg, and cheese?

Curtis *ignores* **Hill**'s *comment.*

Curtis   Come on, Tonya, tell me you see it too . . . It's about as subtle as this bench where we used to sit our chairs, and it's as blatant as that new building across the street . . . they've been doing construction for two years, and now without announcement, or warning, white folks showing up with boxes and we didn't get the invite . . .

Tonya   Mr. Curtis . . .

Curtis   Tonya, they don't sell quarter bags of chips anymore!

Tonya   No more Lays, Doritos, or Utz?

Hill   Gone.

Tonya   What about my "Takis"?

Hill   Gone, girl. Gone!

He tries to hand **Tonya** *the brown paper bag.* **Tonya** *just gives him a look.*

I'll take a sip for you . . .

He sips from the brown paper bag.

White people gon' make you drink eventually. They always doing white people type shit. They move in and invade your territory until where you were ain't where you are. First, they buy your neighbor out, then they raise the rent on Joe's storefront, then they stop Mo from getting his liquor license renewed, then they take the staple chips right out of your corner bodega. Tactical with it.

Tonya   You make change sound like war.

Curtis   Well, ain't that what it is?

Hill   HAVES VERSUS HAVE-NOTS.

Curtis   Right.

Hill   WHITE VERSUS BLACK.

Curtis   DAMN RIGHT.

Tonya   Okay, Farrakhan, so how come you two didn't fight back?

Curtis   With what?!

Tonya   Maybe something more than just words.

Curtis   You make it sound like we had a choice, or that we saw different ways to resist. We didn't have options, Tonya.

Tonya   There's always options, Mr. Curtis.

Curtis   Black folks can only be but so creative in our survival. A syrup sandwich can feed you, but don't mean you gone be fed right. When you have resources, you can move as you like, you can strategize, plan the future, but when you too busy surviving most days, you don't have room for plans. You gotta take care of right now, in the moment, even if it ain't much . . . it's all you can afford to be responsible for.

Tonya   I hear that but isn't there something you could've done?

Hill   He just told you. Survive.

Tonya   I get that, but what about pooling your money together and buying back the block?

Hill   With First and Fifteenth money? Denied. Denied. Denied.

Tonya   This is America, money is money.

Hill   But white money is long and approved; black money is limited and suspect. If they look at us funny, how you think they look at our money? Emir ain't never looked at us like he do these white folks. He's watched too many of us barely make it. Survival is a means for exploitation, not exchange. It's hard to respect people you can take advantage of . . . but when you want someone to respect you, you'll get dolled up, and do things to accommodate them, even if it means raising prices and decreasing the niggas in your shop.

Tonya   But I'm a customer too. I'm paying money just like anyone else. My Black dollar has value, and I can do more than just sit outside and complain, no offense Mr. Curtis.

Hill   This new generation, boy; No respect for the elders.

Curtis   Baby girl, more is not our responsibility, that's yours. We did all we could, and all it got us was this. The choice to remain, to sit in the shade and talk junk, and if God is in a good mood, we can get a game of bones or spades happening without trouble or bad news finding us before we count our books.

Tonya   Mr. Curtis, I hear you. I really do. And maybe this is what we need more of, conversations across the generations, but if you think I'm in a position to buy back the block as a freelance writer, I hate to disappoint you, but I ain't got it. I'm working on it, but it's just as hard for me.

Curtis   But at least you got vision. You can see your way and it ain't some far-fetched dream. Dreams only come true for a few. But it's the ones with vision, a plan, choices. That's what makes your generation different than ours. We grew up on faith and hope—God rest her soul, every word out my mama's mouth was soaked in faith . . . hope, a home in heaven after we leave this hell. But nobody gave us the choice to enjoy reality. We had to find our way in the dark. We labored in the fields, the plants, scrubbing other people's floors, collecting not-for-nothing jobs so you could get beyond hope.

Tonya   Why you hating on hope, Mr. Curtis? A Black man ran on hope and he got eight years in the White House.

Hill   Don't get him started on that nigga.

Curtis   Most times hope is just used to escape the mess you in cause you can't see a way out. Hope will blind you from reality. It happened to Obama's ass too. But vision . . . vision articulates a future while understanding the present. Now you tell me what kind of future is in store for the Stuy? What are these white folks articulating about tomorrow? Who shops at Emir's bodega in the future?

Tonya   Me . . . and all my friends.

Hill   Tonya, what your friends look like?

Curtis   You being delusional, little sister.

Tonya   Delusional, Mr. Curtis? Really?

Curtis   You're only thinking about what you can afford, and not what is being offered to you. You think it's an achievement to be able to buy something from someone that don't want you to have it. You can't just think about yourself. What about me, Tonya? What about all of us, not just a few of us? What about the Black folks who been here hoping for change to come before you and all your bougie friends moved here.

Tonya   Now I may brunch on the weekend and enjoy a good mimosa, Mr. Curtis, but I aint bougie. And I moved here when white people still thought it was dangerous. Bed Stuy went from down and out to up-and-coming overnight. I wanted to be here, because it looked like the Southside of Chicago. It may not have everything, but it does have us, and that was safe enough for me.

Hill   That's beautiful, Tonya. Really. And you said something that I want to go back to. What's a mimosa? Is that Mexican, like an enchilada?

Tonya   It's a drink, Hill. Orange juice and Champagne.

Hill   Ugggh. That sound like some white people shit. Curtis, maybe we wasting our breath . . . I mean the girl got the nerve to be working for free, and tellin' people about it.

Tonya   Sir. No. Freelance means I work with companies when I choose to.

Hill   So you run your own business.

Tonya   Basically, yes.

Hill   Ain't that an entrepreneur?

Tonya   Yes, but . . .

Hill   So why not just say that? You not a businessman, You a business, man.

Tonya   That's wo-man.

Hill (*flirtatious*)   And if you were my woman, you could freelance with me any time you want.

Tonya   Sir. If you don't focus. You keep taking us on these little tangents.

Hill   Alright. Alright. I'mma go in here and grab an Arizona, Miss Tonya, you got me thirsty as hell. Y'all want something?

Tonya   If you don't mind, I wanted to see if they had "pop-chips"?

Hill Well, of course. They ain't change that much. But which one you want? Soda, chips or both . . .

Tonya No. Pop. Chips.

Hill I heard you the first time. And this is New York we don't say pop, it's soda. But you still ain't told me what kind you want.

Tonya It's a brand, Hill. Popcorn in the shape of chips.

Hill Ohhhhhhh. See that's just stupid. White people always fucking with some shit. You might be too bougie for me.

He walks toward the bodega disgruntled.

Curtis, dog you straight?

He turns to look back, but **Curtis** *waves off the request.* **Hill** *continues inside.*

Emir, man, cut this got damn doorbell off!

Tonya Am I really bougie?

Curtis Look, Miss Tonya, you alright with me. Just don't get confused by all the new and shiny. Just because the Stuy is trending now, don't mean everything is looking up for everybody. Some of us only get enough to remain, and there is value in staying power, holding on; me carrying it until you take it further. You need my history of this neighborhood so that you can see its future. And you can't stop at money—money didn't save Joe's Hightower's laundromat, and all the money I spent here didn't save my favorite chips. But you, you got more access than we ever had, but you need perspective. Money is just maintenance, but perspective is how you sustain.

Hill *comes out of the store smacking on chips.*

Hill Curt, you won't believe this! They don't sell Arizonas no more either. This boy Emir tried to sell me some Kombu-chaka-laka, talking about it's the same thing. It ain't the same damn price! Ten dollas fa' some tea that look like it got backwash sitting at the bottom of it.

Tonya It's called Kombucha. And it's better for you.

Hill Shit ain't better for my pockets—But these Kettle chips though! They straight.

Curtis You paid fo' dollas for dem chips?

Hill Hell naw, Curt. I grabbed them and walked out. Told that nigga to put it on my tab. You don't ask for reparations, you take 'em.

Tonya *and* **Curtis** *share a chuckle about* **Hill.**

Tonya Perspective.

Curtis Perspective.

Section 6

The Black Family: How We Thrive in the Face of Oppression

For all the challenges outlined and dramatized in the preceding chapters, the Black community's struggles with equality in representation, education, resources, and systemic racism, Blacks have continued to strive and make progress. Much of our ability to continue pushing forward in the face of extreme obstacles is due to our greatest asset—the Black family. The Black family and community are the cornerstones of Black life in America. The bond of the Black family is at the heart of our survival through generations of oppression and has been the key to our gains both personally and collectively. Over the years, The Fire This Time's stages have portrayed the beauty and strength of the Black family. In the following plays, Camille Darby's *Exodus*, Marcus Gardley's *The Sporting Life of Icarus Jones*, Charly Evon Simpson's *The House*, Kendra Augustin's *Sisterhood in the Time of the Apocalypse*, and Samantha Godfrey's *C.O.G.s*, we see Black family life that reflects the tough love, tenderness, education, acceptance, and strength of bonds that build up Black bodies to be courageous enough to walk through a hostile world outside their homes.

Foreword by Ngozi Anywanyu, The Fire This Time's New Works lab alumnus, prolific writer, and playwright of NYT Critic's Pick *Homecoming Queen*, a play about the bonds of family, history, and ritual

There are steps I'm told.
To how this life is supposed to go.
I am told before I came to this world.
My parents met.
The circumstances are hazy
Debatable even
But somehow led to me.
If I am to believe my own myth
When we are born . . .
If we are lucky, we come out of the womb and then we are welcomed to home of
sorts . . . And what proceeds after that is a crapshoot . . .
A welcoming
maybe a christening if you're lucky
A hazing to most and you're met with the barrage of adolescence and expectations of
the people who decided to bring you into this world or so-call take you in
And we are given advice by these people these people we call our caretakers
Our parents
And to some of us if we are lucky
These people are known as family If unlucky, overseers
And we are met with their expectations their demands
Their baggage, their triggers, their trauma Which leads to their advice . . .

All in one and we grow into the adults who become and realize that we are them for better or for worse and then if we are lucky or in some cases unlucky depending on how you look at it
we continue the cycle again and we give birth or we give care the best way we know how,

And we continue
This cycle
Be it vicious or glorious
For however long we can
And this is family.
Maybe . . .
Anyway the playwrights.

Play #16: Exodus *by Camille Darby*

A mother and daughter finally try to resolve their differences . . . before it's too late.

Presented in The Fire This Time Festival Season 2, directed by Christopher Burris, performed by Angela Polite (**Catherine**) and Lisa Rosetta Strum (**Janet**).

Characters

Catherine, *Black woman, mother, eighties.*
Janet, *Black woman, daughter, thirties.*

Place

The kitchen table inside a small apartment.

Exodus: A Short Play *by Camille Darby*

Music with the mood and energy of a song like "Black is the Color" by Nina Simone is played against a dark stage.

Lights up.

Evening. **Catherine** *sits at small table in the kitchen. Two empty chairs surround her.*

Catherine   Those ol' dried up plants finally stopped holding on. I can't say I'm sad about it. This little apartment is no place to grow anything anyway . . . poor little leaves don't stand a chance. Not like our garden back at the house, right? We grew everything back there. Tomatoes, callaloo . . . remember that squash?

She waits for a response.

Yes!

Laughing.

Yes . . . it was beautiful. Dinner was good that evening.

Janet, *her daughter, enters.*

Janet   Mama, why don't you turn on some more light?

She removes her coat and hangs it over a chair. She moves over to the window to open the shades. **Catherine** *notices* **Janet**, *disappointed that she has been interrupted.*

Catherine   I can see. Have all the light I need.

Janet   You talking to papa again? It's been twenty-five years.

Catherine Twenty-six. Shame . . . you don't even know when your own father died. Just because the death was sudden doesn't mean—

Janet I miss him too, Mama, and I didn't—

Catherine You forgot.

Janet I can't carry that pain. We have to live with what we know. Reality. Life goes on.

Catherine For you.

Janet Don't you think you should use your time to—

Catherine To what? Sit here, rot to death and have you and your brother bury me in a cemetery along the freeway where the dirt is hard and cold? You know I need to be buried next to your father, at home.

Janet *approaches* **Catherine**.

Janet You're tired. Let me help you to bed. We have a busy day tomorrow.

Beat.

Janet (*off* **Catherine**'s *silence*) We're moving you out of here.

Catherine *takes a moment. Overwhelmed with joy, she looks over at* **Janet** *with a broad smile. She tightens her small hands into fists, shaking them in the air.*

Catherine Thank you, Jesus! Finally! What was it? What changed?

Janet I knew you never loved the place, but I didn't expect this kind of reaction.
Catherine *reaches over placing her hand on* **Janet**'s.

Catherine This is the best news I've heard in years.

Janet It's not like the house back home, but I thought it was the closest thing to it for where we are. You will have more space, a backyard—

Catherine I never planned to stay here forever. You know I don't like flying, but I've never been happier at the thought of getting on a plane.

Janet Flying?

Catherine How're we getting there then? Banana boat?

Janet Oh Lord, Mama. We've gone over this. We're not going to the old house. You can't live there by yourself.

Catherine I am here by myself.

Janet Yes, but at least we're all in the same country. The whole family is here now; just a phone call and a drive away. If you live back home and something happens to you, how can we get to you in time? It's just not comforting to know you're there by yourself.

Catherine   Comforting for who? If we're not going home . . . to my home . . . then where the hell are we going?

A moment.

Janet   Henry and I wanted to talk to you together, but he's gone for the next few days for work.

Catherine   Call him then. That's why you got that black ringy thing for, isn't it?

Janet   We decided that you should move in with me, Kelly and Rich.

Catherine   To your house? What does Richard have to say about this?

Janet   I mentioned it to him. He'll be OK with whatever the details are.

Catherine   He's the head of the household. This type of thing requires a discussion, not a mention in passing.

Janet   I know what I'm doing, Mama. I don't want a lecture tonight.

Catherine   Oh, so you come in here interrupting my evening with you and your brother's bright idea, I tell you what I think about it, and now you don't want to hear it?

Janet   This is a family matter. I don't necessarily need Rich's approval here.

Catherine   So husbands aren't a part of the family these days?

Janet   I didn't mean it that way. You're just as much a mother to him as you are to me, which is why I know he'll be OK with it. Just the other day, he was telling me he'd like to see you more.

Catherine   I'm sure he would, but between you and Kelly, he's got enough women in his house. You think I don't see what you're doing?

Janet   Please, not tonight.

Catherine   You're punishing him. Your father did some things that didn't make me happy, but I didn't punish him.

Janet   He had a heart attack before you had a chance to.

She grabs a cup from the table and walks over to the window to water the dying potted plant; but stops in her tracks.

I'm sorry.

Catherine   You better act like you have some sense.

Janet   The world is different now. There's more to have.

Catherine   What's more to have than love? Forgive that man and move on.

Janet   I'm maintaining. That's the max I can do right now. Besides, I didn't come to talk about Rich. You have to come live with us now. That's what I'm here to discuss with you.

Catherine   This is hardly a discussion, Janet. A discussion would have included you asking me my thoughts. What I want.

Not you and your brother worrying about what's wrong with me and rushing me to lie down when I'm not even tired.

Janet   We've tried to talk to you about this countless times. You won't hear it.

Catherine   For good reason. I've got my own plans anyhow. Me and your father.

Janet   You cannot stay there alone.

Catherine   Don't you think I've been uprooted enough? I left a good place to come here for you and Henry after your father died so you two could have better opportunities. Now you've both made it. Send me home and leave me be.

Janet   What plans are you talking about?

Catherine   They do not concern you.

Janet   We want you to be happy, Mama.

Catherine   You and your brother are living your lives. You both got your families, your friends. What do I have but this empty space and my memories, which according to you is going just as quickly as my sight and this ol' knee? I'm not moving into you and your husband's house, Janet.

Janet   I'm not really asking. It's pretty much a done deal. Besides, Henry and I decided that it's not really cost effective.

Catherine   Have I ever asked you or your brother for anything other than a plane ticket? I hate this place. You put those raggedy little potted plants by my window and call it a garden, and for what? I'm supposed to be happy with that? Think of home with your father and smile? I can't get my hands and knees in the dirt.

Janet   Is that why you let them all die?

Catherine   Everything else is dead around here. Sounds like I might be next if I stay here any longer. Unless the next words out of your mouth are about me going home . . . and I mean my own home . . . I don't want to hear anything else about this.

Janet *moves around the apartment pointing out what needs to be removed.*

Janet   We need to be out by the morning. We can start with your clothes tonight. The movers are coming tomorrow to get all this stuff and put it in storage. I'll come back later to clean up. The broker called me this morning. The new tenants want to move in by the end of the month. Do you hear me? Are you taking what the doctor gave you for that knee?

Catherine   I haven't seen anyone come in and out of here to look at the place. How are people moving in without seeing it?

Janet   It's fine, Mama. Don't worry about it.

Catherine   I may hate the place, but I still live here. What you're saying makes no sense.

Catherine   *takes two bottles of pills from her housecoat, placing them on the table.*

Come. Tell me what this one says.

Janet *re-enters the kitchen.*

Janet   Naproxen.

Catherine   Oh, it's not time to take that one yet. (*Reaching for a different bottle.*) This is the one I want. Here, take a couple of pills for yourself, maybe it'll help ease your own pain.

Janet *slams the bottle of pills on the table.*

Janet (*looking around at* **Catherine**'s *belongings*)   I think we can put these things in storage. The dining table, the breakfront cabinet—

Catherine   There's only one thing worse than staying here, and that's watching you keep up appearances. You must think I'm a fool. Of course you're concerned about this ol' sick knee and bad sight and whatever else is wrong with me because at least it gets your mind off who's really got the illness.

Janet   I am not going to be Rich's doormat, the same way you were Papa's. I don't want that kind of life.

Silence.

Catherine   What kind of life, Janet? A good one?

Were you hungry?

Janet *shakes her head.*

Were you barefoot and cold?

Janet *shakes her head again.*

Speak up.

Janet   No, ma'am.

Catherine   Did we beat you and tell you that you weren't worth a damn?

Janet   No, ma'am.

Catherine   Learn this: there are things greater than you, and if you love those things, you live for them. For better or for worse. Bottom line.

Janet   I stayed with Rich.

Catherine   You've got to do more than that, my child.

Janet   What, sing his praises every night?

Catherine   Yes.

Janet   No. Not me. The moment has passed.

Catherine   You let it.

Janet   There was no other choice.

Catherine   There's always a choice. There's been no other man in my life besides your father. That is a choice.

Janet   How is that fair to you?

Catherine   I don't need anyone else. Not right after he died, and definitely not now. He's enough. Dead or alive. You're lucky enough to have Richard in the flesh.

Janet   I'm doing my part. When does he become accountable?

Catherine   Well, it can't be now, after all these years in marriage and a teenage daughter. You better stop expecting him to owe you something. You decided to stay.

Janet   No, I didn't decide. You told me to.

Catherine   Women hold the family together. That is your job. Do it.

Janet   Please, Mama. No more.

Catherine   Say a prayer and let it go.

Janet   You talk to papa every night as if he was right in front of you. Is that you letting go?

Catherine   Do I sound angry when I speak to him? In fact, don't I seem to be the happiest?

Janet   But he's gone.

Catherine   That's how you choose to look at it.

Janet   This is silly.

Catherine   OK. Fine. I won't say anything else about it.

A moment.

Since I have to be out of here tomorrow, let me have this night alone. As much as I hate this apartment, I still need to say goodbye. Get some things together.

Janet   I can help you with that.

Catherine   Janet.

Janet   OK.

She grabs her coat.

I'll see you in the morning.

Catherine   Mmmhmm.

Janet   Have a good night . . . I'm sorry for what I said.

She kisses **Catherine***'s cheek.*

Catherine   I know.

Janet *exits.*

Catherine   Your kids are working my nerves, Joe. Might have to find my own way to you . . . one way or another.

Music with the mood and energy of a song like "When I Fall in Love" by Betty Carter comes in.

Catherine *finally rises from the table. Using her cane, she walks slowly to the window. For the first time, the audience sees the extent of her physical illness. She struggles in the short journey to the window, folding her lips tightly. She takes the cup from the window sill.*

The walk back to her seat at the table is still no easy feat, but she makes it.

Sitting, she takes one bottle, opens it, then opens the next mixing the pills into one bottle. With a gentle shake, **Catherine** *looks over at the empty chair. Her husband's chair.*

She re-opens the bottle, pouring a few pills into her frail hand, then finally throws them back. She sips from the cup. Looking over at her husband's chair again, she smiles.

Lights fade

Play #17: The Sporting Life of Icarus Jones
by Marcus Gardley

The myth of Icarus re-told through the life of a young man discovering his sexuality.

Presented in The Fire This Time Festival Season 2, directed by Lynda Gravatt, performed by Clinton Roane (**Icarus Jones**), Stanley W. Mathis (**Deadlust Jones**), and Zurin Villanueva (**Nurse/Songstress/Narrator**).

Characters

Deadlust Jones, *handyman and super from the South. Not the best father but his intentions are good; an alcoholic.*
Icarus Jones, *his son, feminine, smart, beautiful and tortured by a world where he can't find his place.*
Songstress/Nurse, *the narrator.*

Place

The hood.

Time

Right now before more gay youth kill themselves.

Note

This is a ten-minute play written for The Fire This Time and Baldwin. And in memory of the many gay youths who flew too close to the sun spiraling from wings of wax. May this flight save at least one.

The Sporting Life of Icarus Jones *by Marcus Gardley*

A shaft of sunlight falls on a stage bare except for an easy chair. Deadlust Jones paces back and forth while a songstress sings offstage.

Songstress

    Night is juba
    Night is conga
    Weaving weariness to make two wings

A **Nurse** *enters holding a wailing baby.*

Nurse   Congratulations, Mr. Jones. You have a healthy, newborn boy. And boy, can he holler.

Deadlust   He get that from his momma. She don't ever hush. Even when she eat, she chew-talkin, and when she sleep, she snorin. Hell, even her clothes be loud. But I love her like butter loves toast. I know I shoulda stayed in the hospital room with her but I just can't bear to see her in pain. How is she? She sounded like she was screamin bloody murder a minute ago.

Nurse   It was a difficult labor. You want to hold the baby.

Deadlust   Nawl. Ain't washed my hands yet. Plus, they trembling: these hands. I might drop him. I'm a handy man but I ain't never held no baby.

Nurse   You gonna have to hold him eventually. What better time than the present to hold a gift. Go on . . . he got your eyes.

Deadlust   Ya don't say.

Nurse   I do. Hold him and see.

She hands him the baby; he takes it slowly.

Deadlust   Well, don't this beat Jesus doing jumpin jacks on the river. He do got my eyes. You gone be finer than coon's fur, just you wait. I'm a have to beat the ladies away with a broom.

The baby laughs.

Hold the hot sauce, he got a sick sense of humor like his pop. Awl, we gone be fine. Did my wife see him? She's got to hear this boy laugh. I got to show her—

Nurse   —No! Mr. Jones. Don't go in there. There's much blood. The doctor's planning on coming out here. He needs to tell you a thing—

Deadlust   Is she alive?

Nurse   The doctor will be here shortly.

Deadlust   I don't want the doctor! Tell me! Is my love alive?

Nurse   There were complications. A choice had to be made, sir. It was either her or the baby and she chose . . . (*Looking at the baby.*) Icarus. That's what she named him before she left. She said to tell you, to keep his feet planted but his head faced toward the sun and he'll soar.

Deadlust *pulls the baby to his face and kneels. The* **Nurse** *moves to comfort him but can't. She walks away as she sings.*

Nurse (*singing*)

Night is a juju man.

Weaving a wish to make two wings . . .

A chime. The **Nurse** *crosses the stage holding a placard:* The Sporting Life of Icarus Jones, Part 1. Seven Years Later: Boxing. *She exits.* **Deadlust** *unravels the blanket* *formed as a baby. He puts it over him, sits and watches TV.* **Icarus**, *seven, enters with a black eye. He tries to sneak past his pop, who sits among empty bottles of beer.*

Icarus   Hey, Pop.

Deadlust   How was school?

Icarus   Educational. How was work?

Deadlust   Shitty. I spent all day fixing Mrs. Crete's toilet on the fourth floor. She said she got up this morning shittin bricks and clogged it. I spent half the day knee deep in her shit and listenin to her bitch about her colon. Like I say, it was a shitty day.

Icarus *almost manages to reach his bedroom.*

Deadlust   How'd you get the black eye?

Icarus   Black eye? What black eye? I don't see no black eye.

Deadlust   Probably cause you can't see. Looks like somebody punched the daylights out of you.

Icarus   No, just had a bad fall. I was walkin and tripped. I be trippin. But I'm alright, Pop. I'm going to bed now.

Deadlust   It's only 5 o'clock and you ain't even ate dinner.

Icarus   I'm not hungry. Goodnight.

Deadlust   Bring me a beer, would ya?

Icarus   Another one? Looks like you've already had plenty.

Deadlust   Icarus. You know how I feel about repeating myself, don't you?

Icarus   Yes, sir.

He hands him a beer. He grabs his son and puts the cold beer on **Icarus**'s *eye.*

Icarus *jumps.*

Icarus   Ow!

Deadlust   If I didn't know better, I'd swear I saw a fist print on your cheek there.

Icarus   No. It's a scar from when I fell.

Deadlust   I'm lookin at knuckle prints.

Icarus   You're probably a lil drunk tho, Pop.

Deadlust   Not too drunk to notice knuckle prints. Never that drunk. Somebody's been punchin they name on your face. I'm not sure if you're aware of it or not cause I know you wouldn't lie to your father. Now would you?

Icarus   He called me a punk. Said I was girly cause I read books and I'm soft cause my clothes match so I slapped him. I slapped him like a punk and he punched me like a bully. It was like an after-school special 'cept in this case the bad guy won.

Deadlust   I blame myself. I should've taught you how to box a long time ago. It's just things have been so crazy down at the shop, and somebody always needin something fixed in this building. But you're the most important thing in my life. I'm gone take care of you. It's time I taught you how to box.

He takes rope from the pockets of his mechanic's uniform. The rope is extremely long and feels like a magic trick. It makes a boxing ring. A bell ring out of the space. A bell rings.

Icarus   Is this really necessary?

Deadlust   There ain't but two types of men that live in the hood, son. One of 'em is dyin to get out and the other's just dyin. I ain't raisin no dead boy. Means you got to learn how to fight. You got to learn how to get out of the box. Go ahead, hit me.

Icarus   Hit you where?

Deadlust   Anywhere. Just knock me one. Good and hard.

Icarus   Awl, man, I'm tired.

Deadlust *slaps him, softly.*

Deadlust   You're not tired, you're weak. Come on . . . spread your arms. I want to see you fly. Dance around . . . like this. Keep your hands protectin your face.

Icarus   Are you for real?

Deadlust *jabs him across the head—hard.*

Icarus   Man, quit playin! Shoo.

Deadlust   Then hit me!

Icarus   You're a drunk, you know that!

Deadlust *hits him again—the hardest!*

Deadlust   Hit me, Icarus! Stop being soft and hit your father!

Icarus *runs toward him and starts jabbin into his gut.* **Deadlust** *cowers over his son, then rises as* **Icarus** *continues to hit him.* **Deadlust** *spreads his arms as if flying and starts to laugh loudly, taking the jabs as if they tickle.*

Deadlust   THERE YOU GO! THERE YOU GO, BABY! NOW YOU'RE A MAN! HUNH! NOW YOU'RE FLYING!

He continues to laugh as **Icarus** *walks away, defeated. A chime. The* **Songstress** *enters with another placard: Part 2. Seven Mo' Years: Fishing. She hands* **Deadlust** *a pole. He sits on his easy chair and fishes.*

Songstress (*singing*)

Drifting in the pines
Night is a wind song

Laughing all the time
What surprise it brings

The **Songstress** *exits as Icarus, fourteen, enters with a pole and a milk crate. He and his father "fish."*

Deadlust Ya bored yet.

Icarus Been bored.

Deadlust Well, that's fishin for ya. Teaches ya patience if nothin else.

Icarus Say, Pop?

Deadlust Yes, Icarus.

Icarus You know this isn't really a fishpond don't you?

Deadlust Course.

Icarus It's a pothole. Full of mud and water. There aren't any fish here. You know that, Pop—right?

Deadlust Course. We're simulatin. I mean we're fishin but we're not really fishin. We're just sittin really. Sittin-fishin. That's what fishin really is anyway. Sittin. I just want us to have the poles out to keep our hands occupied. Ain't it nice though? This.

Icarus It's strange. Makes me wonder if you should see somebody. I mean we're sittin in an empty parkin lot holdin fishin poles over a pothole. That ain't normal. You know that, Pop—right?

Deadlust Just imagine. It ain't fishin less you imagine, Ik. This is nice though, hunh? This.

Icarus It's what old men do. Old white men.

Deadlust It's what fathers and sons do.

Icarus Old white fathers and sons, Pop.

Deadlust That's not true. Me and my daddy used to fish all the time when I was your age. Mean, we wouldn't talk like me and you. That's cause we didn't have the healthy relationship you and I got. But me and my daddy used to sit and fish almost every other Sunday after church. Even in our dress clothes. Course we'ze country folks and you a city boy, which is why we usin puddles instead of real ponds here.

Icarus Potholes, Pop. Not puddles. Potholes.

Deadlust Yeah but it's nice though. And serene, isn't it? The scenery. Everything in nature is of God and serene. So, how's everything? In your life? How's life and things?

Time.

Icarus Oh God. You're about to talk about the birds and the bees' nest aren't you.

Deadlust The birds and the who . . .?

Icarus   The birds and the bees' nest. This one of those scary ass comin of age talks isn't it?

Deadlust   Look, I found a condom in your pants pocket when I was doing laundry—

Icarus   —Oh God, Pop!—

Deadlust   —Don't "Oh, God" me. You the one getting your freak on. I didn't want have to do this. It's my job. You the one sexually attractive.

Icarus   Active. It's sexually active.

Deadlust   Yeah, that too. Are ya? Are ya any of those?

Icarus   I'm fourteen.

Deadlust   What that mean? Is that a no? It sounds like a no.

Icarus   I'm fourteen. Of course I'm sexually active. I'm practically a man.

Deadlust   What? Where? When? Who? How? Why?

Icarus   Pop, you got to calm down.

Deadlust   You calm down! How the hell you become sexually attractive?! Oh Lord, everything's serene . . . everything in nature is of God and serene. How long have ya been gettin busy for?

Icarus   A couple of months.

Deadlust   And is she a Christian girl? Is she saved, sanctified, filled with the Holy Ghost? Can she read?—

Icarus   —Who said it was a girl?

Dead silence. **Deadlust** *laughs up a storm.*

Deadlust   That was a good one! Ha! You got me. Almost made me shit on myself. *Who said it was a girl.* Course it's a girl. Like I'm suppose to believe—

Icarus   —Everything in nature is serene, Pop. Everything in nature is of God and serene.

Deadlust *stares at his son. More dead silence.*

Deadlust (*well paced*)   Fuck. Shit. Damn. Fuck. Oh, shit. Fuck-shit-damn. But it's cool. You punkish: that's cool. I mean, I don't prefer it but . . . who gives a fuck who you fuck, shit. I still love you, damn. Fuck, you growin up so quick . . . shit. What the fuck.

Icarus *tears up.* **Deadlust** *drops his pole and awkwardly tries to wraps his son in an embrace.* **Icarus** *moves to avoid it.*

Icarus   Wait! I think I caught somethin.

Deadlust   What? Well, reel it in boy. Reel it in.

Icarus *reels in his line. There is actually a small fish at the end of it.*

Icarus   Jesus, Pop. I think it's a fish.

A chime. **Icarus** *exits. The* **Songstress** *enters with a placard:* Part 3. Even Seven Mo' Years: Baseball.

Songstress (*singing*)

Momma flew back to Africa
She spread her arms flew away
Singing night is juba
Night is Congo
Weaving a wish to make two wings

Deadlust *picks up a bat and practices his swing. He is drunk, worried.* **Icarus** *enters, twenty-one. He is high and wet with self-loathing.*

Deadlust   Where you been?

Icarus   Out.

Deadlust   You look like you're out of your head? You been smokin that mary-don't-wantcha, ain'tha?

Icarus   Better to be high than wasted.

Deadlust   Watch your mouth, I'm still your father.

Icarus   Then you should be proud. Like father like son. Putting our demons down with spirits and herbs.

Deadlust *opens another can of beer.*

Deadlust   I won't have this: you stayin out all night, goin to them clubs, then comin home high on yourself or somebody else and talkin down to me like I'm spit. This ain't you. If you're going out there to find yourself, be careful what part you bring back cause all of you is bout to get your ass kicked.

Icarus   Go ahead, Pop. Pop me. After all these years of being bullied I've learned how to take a hit. See if I even bleed at this point.

Deadlust   You know I did the best I can, I tried to teach you how to defend yourself . . .

Icarus   But I still remained soft, didn't I.

Deadlust   I never said that.

Icarus   —You don't need to say it. Your eyes are loud. You cringe when I hang my wrist, when I cross my legs, when I stare at other men.

Deadlust   I'm going to bed. I've heard enough of this shit.

He gets to his bedroom door.

Icarus   I took a lot of pills, Pop. Cause I want to soar. Tonight. I want to touch the sun as he lays over the horizon.

He stands on the easy chair. He spreads his arms. Then slumps in the chair with a loud thud then falls to the floor. **Deadlust** *runs in, sees him passed out.*

Deadlust   Icarus? Icarus, what have you done?

Icarus (*fading*)   Don't be mad at this body. It can't help but be soft. For you and my mother made it fine as silk. And this voice, it can't help but be high: for you and my mother gave me the song of angels. These hips that sway and this heart that loves men–they too are innocent. For the sway was cut from the oceans and the heart pumped from rivers deep in yours and my mother's blood. This body that you made . . . is beautiful. (*He tears up.*) I just can't live in it no more. It's too hard.

He falls into a coma.

Deadlust   Son, you wake up. What, did you take son?! I'm not letting you leave here! Icarus, wake up!

He picks up his son and gets behind him as if to give the Heimlich maneuver. He pumps air into his son.

Songstress (*singing*)

> Drifting in the windy pine
> Night is a song, a lullaby

Deadlust   I know you see that light but don't you go near it. It'll burn you.

Songstress

> Laughing wild and all the time.

Deadlust   You hear me, Icarus! You stay here. With me!

Songstress

> Night is a mourning juju man.

Deadlust   I don't care how you're made. You're mine, boy.

Songstress

> Weaving a wish and weariness.

Deadlust   Come back to me.

Icarus *lifts his arms.*

Songstress

> To make.

Deadlust   COME ON! COME ON!

Icarus' *arms flap.*

Songstress

Today!

Deadlust   That's it! Come home.

Icarus *arcs his back and flies.*

Songstress

. . . New wings.

Deadlust   From now on, me and you, we fly together!

Icarus *opens his eyes and breathes air as if to release the poison in his body. The wind blows out the sun.*

Lights out.

Play #18: The House *by Charly Evon Simpson*

The need to decide what to do with their father's house brings siblings Brian and Jackie together on a cold winter afternoon.

Presented in The Fire This Time Festival Season 9, directed by Candis C. Jones, performed by Corey Allen (**Brian**), and Erin Cherry (**Jackie**).

Characters

Brian, *Black man, mid-thirties. Put together and practical.*
Jackie, *Black woman, early thirties. More of a free spirit.*

They are siblings.

Place

Outside their father's house. In the New Jersey suburbs.

Time

Winter 2016. A cold afternoon.

The House *by Charly Evon Simpson*

When the lights come up, the stage is quiet.

Brian *stands center stage, facing the audience.*

He is wrapped up in a winter coat.

He keeps his eyes forward and his arms crossed. We don't see it, but **Brian** *is staring at a big house that's old and light green and has white trim.*

He is waiting.

After some time, **Jackie** *enters behind him.*

She is also wrapped up warmly but everything she wears is colorful and looks like she could have knitted it herself.

She is quiet. **Brian** *doesn't notice her.*

She gets very close behind him, so close we wonder how he doesn't know she's there.

After a few beats, she breathes a little heavier. It is **Jackie**'s *breath that gives her away.*

Brian *feels it on his neck and so he jumps.*

Brian   Jack!

Jackie   What?

Brian   You scared me. You didn't fucking say / anything.

Jackie   Sorry.

Brian   I could feel you. Like your breath. On my neck.

A moment.

Then he mumbles to himself.

Ever since you came back from the damn woods . . .

Jackie   What?

Brian   Nothing. So, the house—

Jackie   Clearly, it's not nothing.

Brian (*sighing*)   It's nothing.

Jackie   Fine. So, the / house . . .

Brian   You're quieter.

Like I could hear your footsteps before and now . . . now I can only feel your breath after you are already here.

You've gotten quieter since you came back from the woods.

Jackie   That was the point.

Brian   What?

Jackie   I went to the woods to get quieter. It was a retreat, B. That's what retreats / are for.

Brian   I'm not an idiot.

Jackie   Then you just don't get it.

Brian   You're right. I have no idea why you'd willingly go to the middle of nowhere to sit in silence for days on end.

Jackie   Because I like nature / and meditation.

Brian   Like how many Black people go to the woods? For good reason. Crazy people live in the woods. People who make their own deodorant and eat only berries live in the woods. People who carry Confederate flags live in the woods. The Klan meets in the woods, Jackie. The Klan.

Jackie   People make deodorant in the city too, B.

He looks at her.

We aren't any safer in the city. If I used your logic, I wouldn't leave my apartment.

Brian   Whatever . . . I'd just . . . I'd like some noise. To alert me. To your presence.

Jackie *exits.*

She then walks back in stomping her feet.

Jackie   Is that better?

Brian   Can we get on with the house? I've been waiting.

Jackie   Fine. Sure. Let's get on with it.

Brian   Okay.

Jackie   Okay.

Brian *points to the house in front of them.*

Brian   What are we going to do with the house?

Jackie   I don't know. What are we going to do with the house?

Brian   We are supposed to figure something out. Together.

Jackie   I thought we'd figure it out after.

Brian   After what?

Jackie   After we looked at it for a while.

Brian   What?

Jackie   Like I thought we'd stand here and look at it for a bit. Then go grab some coffee or something and see how we felt.

Brian   Maybe you should move permanently to the woods, Jack. Maybe you belong there.

Jackie   If only I could.

Brian   Please . . . can we just make some decisions now?

Jackie   You're tense.

Brian   Not all of us can just go ignore all our responsibilities while communing—

Jackie   You said I could go.

Brian   Yeah . . .

Jackie   You said that I *should* go. That we could figure all of this out when I got home.

Brian   I know.

Jackie   So, don't hold it against me for God's sake.

She stares toward the house.

I don't want the house, B. You can have it if you want. I'm not going to fight about it.

Brian   I don't want it either.

Jackie   Oh.

Really?

Brian   Yeah. You're surprised?

Jackie   Yeah. I thought you'd want to . . . to . . . like . . . raise your family in it.

Brian   Not sure it holds the right memories for that.

Jackie   I mean, yeah. Yeah.

So.

We sell it?

Brian   Yeah. We sell it.

They stare at the house.

Jackie   Is that it?

Brian   Yes . . . I mean we have to actually sell it, but yes.

There is a cold wind that blows and they hug themselves a bit tighter.

Jackie *keeps looking ahead at the house.*

Jackie   I still find it spooky.

Brian   It's not spooky. Filled with bad memories, yes. Spooky, no.

Jackie   It totally is. And was. And is all those things.

Brian   You just have an overactive imagination.

Jackie   That is what they tell kids so they'll fall in line and become automatons.

Brian   Or because / it's true.

Jackie   The house had secret passageways and hiding places. Little places where something would catch you off guard. It gave me the creeps.

Brian *looks at her.*

Jackie   Don't look at me like that. I mean, it used to hide slaves. How is that not spooky?

Brian   Then according to you the entire South is spooky.

Jackie   Kind of like how all woods are spooky?

A moment.

Brian   You just thought Dad was scary growing up.

Jackie   I wasn't the only one who felt that way. Others said there were things like—

Brian   I know what they said.

Jackie   Like all the cans of food past the expiration date . . .

Brian   That's not spook—

Jackie   No but it helped the vibe. That and the old cookies.

Brian   Dad wasn't good at grocery / shopping.

Jackie   And the sense of lingering ghost folks and the coldness.

Brian   That you say you felt.

Jackie   Others said it too.

Brian   Okay, fine, the house was weird.

Jackie   But you felt it too. I know you did. That's why you didn't visit it or him either . . .

A small moment.

Brian   Do you want to go in? The ghosts won't even know we're there.

Jackie   Do we have to go in now?

Brian   No. Not now. Eventually but—

Jackie   Okay. I don't want to go in.

Brian   Okay.

A moment.

Jackie   The dining table was really long. I don't think the table would really fit any place else. Like it's too long for most houses.

Brian   And we never sat at it. Except that one Thanksgiving.

Jackie   Except that one.

I don't even think we could get it out. Of the house. Without breaking it.

Brian   So we sell it too?

Jackie   Yeah. We sell it. And the house.

Brian   And the house.

Jackie   Yeah.

Brian   Yeah.

They nod to themselves.

Brian *turns away from the house.*

After one last look, **Jackie** *turns as well.*

Brian   What else has changed since you came back from the woods?

Jackie   My hands swell more easily.

Brian   Really?

Jackie   Or maybe I just noticed for the first time.

Brian   Dad would've hated you going on that retreat. And this quiet thing you've got going.

Jackie   Yeah, well, he would've hated the flowers you chose for his funeral so . . .

Brian   They matched the house.

Brian *slowly, quietly, exits.*

Jackie *takes a moment, looks at the house, and then follows.*

Blackout.

Play #19: Sisterhood in the Time of the Apocalypse *by Kendra Augustin*

Two estranged sisters refuse to let anything derail the opportunity to bond with each other—including the impending apocalypse.

Presented in The Fire This Time Season 10, directed by Kevin R. Free, performed by Dana Costello (**Annie**) and Margaret Ivey (**Margaret**).

Characters

Annie, *early to mid-twenties.*
Margaret, *late twenties to early thirties.*

Setting

Hot air balloon in the sky.

Sisterhood in the Time of the Apocalypse *by Kendra Augustin*

Margaret *and* **Annie** *are spending the day in a hot air balloon.* **Annie** *waves below at the guys who helped them get the hot air balloon off the ground.*

Annie   Thanks for helping us with the lift-off, guys. It was nice knowing you.

Margaret   I never pegged you for a hot air balloon type of gal. I am impressed you know how to work one.

Annie   Well, I don't know how to drive a car, or fly a plane, so this seemed like the next logical step, especially since they're all that's left.

Margaret   I just figured you'd be a tea and finger cakes kind of girl.

Annie   I wear many different hats, Margaret. For instance, a few years ago I decided I wanted to be a clown and I just became a clown.

Margaret   How does one become a clown?

Annie   You take classes. Join the circus. Working a hot air balloon makes sense for a clown even though it's not in the manual. Imagine if I was a by the book kind of girl.

Sound of bombs in the distance.

Margaret   It's funny, Annie. I lived my whole life super-scared to die, trying really hard not to die, and now?

Annie   We think we control things, but we don't. We're two in several billion people. We're nobodies.

Annie *pulls out a clown nose from her bag. She puts it on her nose, and it makes a honking noise.*

Margaret   I wouldn't say we're nobodies.

Annie   Maybe you aren't. I definitely was. Am.

Margaret *is silent.*

Annie *does not look at her. She removes her clown nose.*

Margaret   I like the sky cloudy. I always hated the sun. It just burns your skin.

Annie   It also gives you Vitamin D and has kept us from another Ice Age, but hey.

Margaret *just stares at her with daggers in her eyes.*

Annie   What? The sun isn't perfect, but it does a lot of good.

Sounds of bombs in the distance.

Annie *takes out a balloon animal: an elephant.*

Annie   Elephants are still your favorite animals, yeah?

Margaret *takes the balloon animal. She plays with it a bit and makes an elephant sound. Annie also makes an elephant sound. They make elephant sounds in unison. The balloon animal slips from Margaret's fingers. It flies backward, blown away by the wind.*

Annie   Nothing gold can stay, eh?

Margaret   Annie. I was selfish. I thought, "Hey, my parents are dead. I'm free to not live under their constraints." I didn't see taking care of you as my problem.

Annie *notices something in the sky.*

Annie   Oh! Look a raven. Or is that a crow? Don't they signify death?

What a dumb question. Of course, they do. I hate asking stupid questions. That's probably why everyone leaves. I'm so annoying. So stupid.

Margaret   I hate seeing you so unconfident. The Annie I know—

Annie   The Annie you know? You literally just met me.

Margaret   Oh, come on. Yes, it's been several years since we've—

Annie   Ten years, but who's counting?

Sound of rain. They both watch as the rain come down.

Margaret   It looks acidic.

She tries to touch the rain, but **Annie** *swats her hand.*

Annie *takes out her cell phone. She surveys it.*

Annie   I hate these things. They exist but people don't know how to use them. Ten years. No phone call. No texts. No e-mail.

She throws it off the hot air balloon.

Margaret   Thank God for newspapers!

Annie   Of course, I find you through a newspaper. You're basically an old person. If I knew Morse code I probably would have found you sooner.

Margaret   You certainly have Dad's sense of humor.

Annie *is kind of taken aback by the comparison.*

Sound of thunder.

Margaret   Oh, look down there. See that?

Annie *looks down but can't quite figure out what she is looking at.*

Margaret   That's our old playground.

Annie   There's barely anything left. How can you tell?

Margaret   The remnants of the numbers where we played hopscotch are still there. The pink one was a number six. I drew that. Go somewhere enough the details don't escape you.

Annie   They've escaped me.

Margaret   To be fair, I left this town at eighteen. I had a lot more time here. Oh, and that's my old high school! I can tell by the pieces of the skull and bones I drew on the wall. Remember how Mom and Dad thought I was a wild child for committing the crime of graffiti!

Annie   It must have been nice to know they cared about your cry for attention. I'm jealous you got to have Mom and Dad for a longer time than I did.

Margaret   I didn't think having a mom and dad was so great then.

Sound of thunder.

Annie   What?

Margaret   In a way, you were lucky they died when you were twelve because you didn't get to hate them.

Annie   What a privileged thing to say!

Margaret   Your last feelings toward them were love. I hated them even after they died. I couldn't remember their love. I wish . . . that I could do it over.

Sounds of bombs getting a little bit closer.

Annie   I brought some drinks with me. Of the alcoholic variety.

Margaret   I don't really drink anymore.

Annie   I didn't bring beer. I brought Champagne.

Margaret   Champagne is still alcohol.

Annie   But the classy kind.

Margaret   You've always known what kind of person I am. Was? Am.

Annie   See what I'm wearing?

Margaret *recognizes it.*

Margaret   That's my old jumper!

Annie   When I was a kid, I idolized you. Thought you were the coolest person in the world. I thought, "Look at this pretty girl. So fashion forward. So autonomous—I can't wait until I can be like her." Even when you ignored me. Even when you left without saying goodbye.

Margaret   Autonomous?

Annie   I was very well read for my age.

Beat.

Margaret   I'm sorry.

Annie   But I think I get it. Why you left. You felt trapped. Mom and Dad wanted you to be safe. Their idea of safe meant locking you in a cage. You wanted to be free; to stay out past 11 pm and hang out with your friends and kiss boys. You wanted to live a full life. They just wanted you to live. But they forgot that they needed to be kept safe too. We should have caged them.

Margaret   You're so wise.

Annie   I'm not wise. I've just seen the ugly side of humanity. Once you see the cancer that is human nature you get to understand people a little bit. Where they're coming from.

Margaret   It doesn't make the terrible things they do okay, though.

The thunder is louder.

Annie, did terrible things ever happen to you?

Annie *picks up a Champagne bottle, uncorks it, and pours Champagne down her throat.*

Margaret   Don't you have any glasses to pour that Champagne into?

Annie   Margaret. We're going to die. At any moment. Screw manners.

Drink!

Margaret   I don't feel comfortable swapping spit with—

Annie   A stranger?

Margaret   Not what I was going to say.

Annie   But we are strangers. I don't know you. You don't know me. The last time we spoke . . . We're definitely not those girls anymore. It's okay if you don't want to drink from me. I can make Jaeger bombs. I want to be blacked out when I die. So it doesn't hurt. I've been taking bartending classes and—

Sounds of bombs get louder. **Margaret** *begins to have a panic attack.*

Annie   Margaret. Are you okay?

Margaret's *panic attack escalates.* **Annie** *kneels next to her and holds her.*

Annie   Margaret. I'm so sorry. I didn't mean to be so mean. How can I help you? Oh, man, I didn't bring any water. I've got vodka. In a rush, I probably thought it was ginger ale.

Annie *starts breathing with* **Margaret** *in the hopes that she will be able to help her remember how to breathe normally again.* **Margaret**'s *panic attack slowly begins to subside.* **Annie** *just holds her.* **Margaret**'s *head is on* **Annie**'s *lap and they are completely silent even after* **Margaret** *seems to be back to calmness.*

Annie   Are you okay?

Margaret   Yeah . . . Annie?

Annie   Yes, Margaret.

Margaret   Are you okay?

Annie   Yeah.

Margaret   Are you okay, Annie?

Annie   I just said I was.

Margaret   Are you okay? Are you okay? Are you okay, Annie? Annie, are you okay? Are you okay Annie?

Annie   Shut up.

Margaret   How often can that organically happen?

Annie   Never. You scared me half to death!

Margaret   Obviously, I am scared to death, too. Here we are on a hot air balloon, you're drinking Champagne and I haven't seen you for so long, but this is it. I see you now. And I'm happy to see you, but the end is literally near, and it just hit me.

Annie   You're slow to process things, I see.

Margaret   I know I left you behind. Mom and Dad are dead. This is the only life we had, and I blew it.

Annie   You don't think heaven exists? Maybe Mom and Dad are up there?

Margaret   There's the twelve-year-old girl I remembered. So hopeful.

Annie   Mom always said that if we believed in God everything would be okay.

Margaret   But our lives, as we know them to be, are over. Like . . . you don't know I was married.

Annie   You totally left that out of the introduction.

Margaret   He's dead. I didn't think it mattered.

Annie   My condolences. How did he die?

Margaret   In the most cliché of ways: he went off to war and never came back. Also, I hate when people say, "My condolences." It's so empty. I prefer, "I'm sorry for your loss."

Annie   "I'm sorry for your loss. You're an orphan, now. Glad, it's not my tragedy."

Margaret   "I'm sorry for your loss. You're a widow now. Glad, it's not my tragedy."

Thunder comes more ferociously.

Beat.

Annie   The kids, all of them, would make fun of me. They used to say I wasn't worth anyone staying.

Margaret   So, that's why no one else is around.

Annie   *gives her "Ha. Ha. Very funny" look.*

Margaret   I'm sorry.

Annie   I prefer, "My condolences."

Flashes of light.

Margaret   It looks like a blitzkrieg. Do you see that?

Annie   I think our time is almost up. I guess if there is one thing I regret it's not having found my soul mate.

Margaret   That's a pity because I found mine.

Annie   Yeah, yeah, yeah, you found your prince early on. When did you meet?

Margaret   We were your age. But when I said I found my soul mate I didn't mean him. I meant you.

Bombs, thunder, sound of rain, flashes of light.

Annie   Me?

Margaret   Yeah, you. It may have taken me years to learn who the love of my life was, but I'm happy that I found her. Love comes when it's meant to.

Sound of sirens.

Annie *and* **Margaret** *hug.*

Annie   You're the love of my life too.

Blackout.

Play #20: C.O.G.s *by Samantha Godfrey*

A young Brooklynite attends a protest rally with her aunt, on a family visit to the "Peach State," but she soon learns how bitter democracy can be in the sweet ol' South.

Presented in The Fire This Time Festival Season 10, directed by Kevin R. Free, performed by Virginia Woodruff (**Auntie Kay**) and Tia DeShazor (**Vanessa**).

Characters

Auntie Kay, *fifties, Black woman.*
Vanessa, *twenties, Black woman.*

Time

Sometime after America started stealing children away from their parents again.

Setting

Atlanta, GA.

Notes on punctuation

. . . = a trail-off of thought.
// = an overlap or interruption of speech by the character with the line or action that follows.
- = words linked with hyphens are to be uttered as one word.
(. . .) = words within parentheses are not to be spoken.

C.O.G.s: A Ten-minute play *by Samantha Godfrey*

Lights up on:

Auntie Kay, *fifties, cultured, refined woman with a youthful, rebellious soul, speaks with a slight Southern accent, enters the room chanting. She's sporting J-Crew casuals from her hat and sunglasses to her stylish fanny pack and clothes. She holds a protest sign that reads, "IF ANY OF YOU HEATHENS CAUSE ONE OF THESE INNOCENT C.O.G.'s TO STUMBLE, YOU WILL DROWN IN HELL," in her hand. She chants to an imaginary beat, still pumped up from the rally.*

Auntie Kay   Whose streets?!

. . .

Our streets!

Kay *puts down her sign, pleased, then rushes off to the bathroom, still chanting.*

In behind her walks a disengaged **Vanessa**, *early twenties, millennial, woman, wearing a backpack and a shirt that reads "EQUALITY." **Vanessa** holds a banana in one hand and a cardboard sign that reads "I SEE HUMANS BUT NO HUMANITY," in the other. She glares at* **Kay***'s sign until* **Kay** *returns.*

Auntie Kay   Whose streets?!

. . .

WHOSE STREETS?!

AUNTIE KAY

Vanessa   Our streets.

Auntie Kay   That's right.

She takes a palm-sized water out of her fanny pack and finishes the bottle.

So that's it?

Vanessa (*to herself mainly*)

Auntie Kay   Let's make this pee break quick. Use the bathroom, grab one of the sandwiches in the fridge, then let's get back out there.

Vanessa   Why? We're just standing out there in the hot sun in front of the detention center, holding up signs, walking around chanting justice jingles.

Auntie Kay   Exhilarating, isn't it?

Vanessa   . . .

Auntie Kay   Being seen and heard. The world is watching.

Vanessa   Why do we need to be seen and heard? The people making these decisions are inside.

Auntie Kay   To be counted.

Vanessa   By who? For what? To do what . . . be taken into consideration?

Beat.

How many shaky videos and dash-cams have we seen and heard?

Auntie Kay   Not talking about that right now. Talking about democracy. People coming from all over Georgia, uniting for one of the most significant protests in history. Marches all over the country.

Vanessa   Why do we have to march to protest?

Auntie Kay   To be included in the final assessment.

Vanessa   Assessment?

Auntie Kay   Vanessa, we're playing our part. The rest of the world thinks we've gone mad, but we're out there to show them that this is still America and we will not sit idly by while that clown with the nuclear code steals children away from their parents.

Vanessa   And yelling and holding signs is going to influence the final outcome?

Auntie Kay   It's a continuous process.

Vanessa *holds up her sign.*

Vanessa   This is not kicking anyone out of office.

Auntie Kay   Vanessa, baby, who's marched on this earth longer?

Vanessa   I just think . . .

Auntie Kay   You think what?

Vanessa *broaches the subject carefully.*

Vanessa   Maybe instead of chanting "No Justice, No Peace" and "Whose Streets" forty times over, it'd be better to demand specific action. Or maybe, it's time to take real action. Something other than wearing out our soles.

Vanessa *motions to her feet.*

Auntie Kay   You mocking Martin?

Vanessa   How does repeating his steps push us forward?

I thought the definition of insanity was doing the same thing over and over but // expecting different results.

Auntie Kay   It's not.

Vanessa   Since when?

Auntie Kay   Insanity is a term for people like your Uncle Bobby who cannot distinguish fantasy from reality.

Vanessa   Like *his* supporters?

She motions to the TV.

Auntie Kay   It's something that gets in the way of being able to conduct daily affairs due to psychosis. But I'm just a therapist. What would I know? (*Shift.*) Turn on the news, darlin.

Vanessa *turns on the TV, then hands* **Kay** *the remote.*

Auntie Kay   Plenty of areas in life require repetition. It's called perseverance.

She watches the television closely while massaging her feet.

Vanessa   My first protest below the line . . . birthplace of civil rights where Dr. King once preached. I was so excited to go, but it was like being drafted to Cleveland without Lebron, LA without Kobe, Chicago without Jordan. There was nothing there. Not even Dr. King's spirit. Just college kids fresh out for the summer or from the Peace Corp, banging djembe drums and putting up tie-dye tents in front of the detention center, shouting, "F—k the police." They weren't even staying on topic. We were supposed to be there in support of the families, instead it felt like . . . like a . . . empty facade. I felt embarrassed to be standing with them. Almost left to go stand with the cops guarding the detention center. Not all of the people behind those walls got locked up by I.C.E. Not all of them are immigrants, but seemed like everybody was taking the whole "silence is consent" message to heart. So eager to start a chant or raise a bull horn, but who's really saying something and who's just making noise?

Auntie Kay   All I see is New York and Los Angeles coverage. (*Kisses her teeth.*)

Vanessa *turns, disappointed* **Auntie Kay** *wasn't listening. She looks toward the TV and gestures* . . .

Vanessa   Is this what democracy looks like?

Auntie Kay   Were you protesting Barack?

Vanessa   No.

Auntie Kay   Progress.

Vanessa   Congress was.

Auntie Kay   Oh there's Atlanta!

Shoot, they're only showing the federal . . . Do you remember when Bush was in office?

Vanessa   I was ten, but I don't remember having to leave school to protest him every week. I remember my teachers rolling their eyes and Mom and Dad cracking jokes, but ain't shit funny now.

Auntie Kay   Vanessa!

Vanessa   . . .

Auntie Kay   Go get a sandwich and put something healthy in that mouth.

She watches the news intently.

They have speakers and more press coverage. Hmm. Should have gone to the federal building.

She checks her watch.

We still have time to get there before John speaks. Have to get a picture with him for my church group.

Vanessa *looks at* **Kay**'s *sign with contempt and whispers to herself.*

Vanessa   Have to change that sign.

Auntie Kay   What was that?

Vanessa   Where does marching get us?

Auntie Kay   I'm not going back and forth with you.

Vanessa   It pacifies us with organized activity. We get distracted with arts 'n' crafts and songs while law makers carry out their same ol' B.S. policies.

Auntie Kay   Got us through Civil Rights and Women's Rights.

Vanessa   Two glowing examples of areas that couldn't use any improvement.

Auntie Kay (*pause*)   Used to be so sweet before you moved up North. Don't forget. We GET to DO THIS.

Vanessa   I'm asking how can we do this better? (*Pause.*) How do we get inside?

Auntie Kay   . . .

Vanessa   Why couldn't we all go protest at the border? Dismantle the cages? What if all these cities converged and met those families at the—

Auntie Kay   Cause that's illegal.

Vanessa   Who gets to decide what's legal? The same ones who sign voter suppression into law?

Auntie Kay   You need to make a new sign. Someone at the federal building already has it.

Vanessa   What?

Auntie Kay *points to the TV.* **Vanessa** *turns to the television. Her face falls.*

Auntie Kay   See it there? "Where is the humanity?"

Vanessa   It's not the same.

Auntie Kay   Same message.

Vanessa   Right.

She puts her sign down and starts to peel the banana.

Beat.

Vanessa   I don't think I'm up for round . . . (two).

Kay *slaps the banana out of her hand.*

Vanessa   Hey!

Auntie Kay   You don't know what they put in that.

Vanessa   Auntie Kay, W.T.H.! It's a banana!

Auntie Kay   A banana you got from a woman walking through that sweaty eighty-four-degrees-in-the-shade-crowd. You can't eat that!

Vanessa   Why did you let me take it?!

Auntie Kay   I was carrying and quoting scripture, what was I supposed to say? No, we do not want any of that palm-sweated fruit you've been carrying around in your bare, dirty hands? I represent the church. One must be gracious.

Vanessa   . . . then change your sign, so you can be yourself.

Auntie Kay   Hush.

She picks it up.

Vanessa   COGS?

Auntie Kay   Wasn't enough room to write it all out, so I improvised.

Vanessa   Improvised? You chopped 'n' screwed the whole Bible verse.

Auntie Kay   Pastors do it all the time.

Vanessa *presses her lips closed so as not to be disrespectful, then . . .*

Vanessa   It was a perfectly good banana.

Auntie Kay   That could have been injected with something. You don't know her and which party she supports.

Vanessa   Clearly she was one of the Goodwill Ambassadors.

Auntie Kay   Why? Because it said so on her shirt?

Vanessa   She was passing out water and fruit.

Auntie Kay *looks at her niece while detaching a mini-sanitizer bottle off of the zip of her fanny pack.*

Auntie Kay   Didn't my sister teach you anything?

Vanessa *uses the sanitizer.* **Kay** *pulls out a baggie from her fanny pack, and picks the banana up off of the floor in a similar fashion to a dog owner picking up shit. She tosses it in the trash.*

Vanessa   This isn't Halloween in Brooklyn.

Auntie Kay   But down here these tricks love to treat. You're in a Red State.

Vanessa   But it's the Bible Belt.

Auntie Kay   Ain't you sweet.

It's the God-Fearing-Gun-Toting-Law-Abiding-Middle-Class-NRACard-Carrying-Christian-State. And don't you forget it.

Vanessa   What about your church group?

Auntie Kay   . . .

Vanessa   Aren't they progressives?

Beat.

Auntie Kay   Let me tell you something bout the South. How many church groups did you see out there protesting?

Vanessa *takes a moment to think.*

Vanessa   There was that Jewish group.

Auntie Kay   I'm talking about the Christians. The Pro-Life, All-Lives Matter, Christians. Did you see them out there?

She points to the television.

Look at the split screen. See any?

Vanessa *scans the TV thoroughly till she comes to a realization.*

Auntie Kay   Exactly . . . Not one, Pro-All-Anything. See I thought things got better. Knew nothing was perfect, cause I've lived in this skin and this body all my life. I know hate covered up doesn't vanish, it dries up and leaves a scar that can't help but show—cause it's on you.

Kay *reveals a scar underneath her necklace.* **Vanessa** *looks.*

Auntie Kay   Member when I first joined this church. His father was my pastor for years until Barack got elected, then something changed in the atmosphere. People's smiles started drying up. A few of us decided to move to the son's church when he branched out. First we were welcomed in love, and it was, "Sister this and Ms. Kay that, but after I joined the Seniors Life Group, that's when I could tell, same old scars . . . After every unarmed shooting it was, "Kay, he should have identified himself. Kay, she should have been more respectful. Kay, they were doing their job." Wasn't long before some went back to his father. Seemed like the rest just joined the group to share their gran-pictures. So when news broke that they were taking these *Children of God* forcefully from their parents, putting them in locked cages . . . I knew that these grandmothers and grandfathers were going to feel something, say something. I knew that was going to be the first matter we prayed about Sunday, but it didn't even come up. Cotton mouths had nothing to say.

Vanessa   Then why go there?

Auntie Kay   Cause it's closer to my house, nicer than all the Black ones in the area, and we are in by nine and out by ten . . . What? I don't deserve a little comfort with my activism?

Vanessa   Why do you want a picture with John Lewis for them?

Kay *picks up her sign and stands on a couch/chair.*

Auntie Kay   Cause I am the thorn in their side to keep them on their toes and remind them, that no matter how comfortable we get, we will keep coming back. We will not skip past outrage. Hurt and despair will not conquer us. Hate won't drive us out, it will move us into protest.

Vanessa *looks at* **Kay**'s *sign.* **Kay** *comes down from the chair studying* **Vanessa**.

Auntie Kay   I embarrass you?

Vanessa   That sign does. Makes you look like one of those Christians at Times Square telling everyone they need to repent.

Vanessa *flips her aunt's sign over and writes on it.*

Vanessa   Why couldn't you just say something like . . . "Free the Children"?

Auntie Kay   That's been said.

Vanessa   Maybe it needs to be said again.

Beat.

Auntie Kay   I can't let these families think God doesn't care.

Vanessa   What if they believe in a different God? Or don't believe at all? You still gonna march for them?

Auntie Kay   . . .

Vanessa   How'd you get that scar?

Auntie Kay *goes off.*

Auntie Kay (*off*)   1966. S.N.C.C.

Kay *returns with an old bullhorn and a sandwich.*

Auntie Kay   Being seen and heard.

She tosses the sandwich to **Vanessa.**

Vanessa   Thanks. You're gonna need a permit for that.

Auntie Kay   It's not for me. It's for you . . . you got something to say?

Vanessa   What about the police?

Auntie Kay   I've got your back. But if they try to take it, pass it to me quickly. I'll give them my horn when they pry it from my cold dead hands.

Vanessa *picks up the signs.* **Kay** *stops her, takes them, and puts them down.*

They exit.

Section 7

Black Love: Why We Hope

Despite the hardships we face, Black people continue to find joy, happiness, and love. We love fiercely, and that love has propelled us forward generation after generation. In this closing chapter we see how Black love is not only a sacred commitment, but an act of ongoing resistance. As we see in these plays, love has been synonymous with our freedom since the time of our enslavement as dramatized in Jonathan Payne's *The Weatherin'*, and we commit to this love even in worlds and a future that exists in our imagination as we see in Tyler English-Beckwith's *Maya and Rivers*. In between, as we see in Fredrica Bailey's *Love and Happiness*, Angelica Chéri's *Slow Gin Fits*, and Josh Wilder's *Gravity*, we love like any other humans, and it is love that gets us through.

Foreword by Julienne Hairston, The Fire This Time Season 6 playwright, and producer

I was tracing my family's genealogy when I came upon the marriage census created in 1865. I honestly wondered why it was so important for a people to not only "jump the broom" while enslaved, but once freed; register their families and state unequivocally their union. The answer I believe is Love. From the beginning of all that there is and ever will be there is Love. It is always the answer, not only creative but an act of creation: "For God so loved the world."

Black Love is the expression of a people's acknowledgment, awareness, and innate knowing of their connection and oneness with the Universal Life Source. From Black Power to Black Lives Matter; from Lois Mailou Jones to Jean-Michel Basquiat; from Willis Richardson to me, Black Love moved nations, empowered the downtrodden and disenfranchised, and inspired cultures from around the world; binding us all together. Black Love is a creating force and the what and why of my writing.

I found a home at The Fire This Time as a playwright in their 6th season. I was immediately embraced, nurtured, inspired, and acknowledged as an artist. I was heard; I could declare unabashedly that I am a writer and I am here. I hope that my writing of our magnificent past, glorious present, and powerful future will embolden the next generation. As a haven for Black expression in all its diverse and non-monolithic thought, sustaining Black culture, community, creativity, and creation, The Fire This Time Festival is the epitome of Black Love.

Play #21: The Weatherin' *by Jonathan Payne*

In 1905, a man recounts a chilling tale that took place decades earlier about the sacrifices that were made for a daring escape from slavery to freedom.

Presented in The Fire This Time Festival Season 5, directed by Lileana Blain-Cruz, performed by Paul Robert Pryce (**Arnold**), Winston Duke (**Edgar**), and Sheria Irving (**Emily**).

Characters

Arnold Gragston *(Black), forty and thirty, male, ploughman; stoic, dark, brooding.*
Edgar Bell *(Black), eighty-four and forty-two, male, fieldhand; nervous, handsome, weak.*
Emily Anderson *(Black), twenty-seven, female, stockwoman; spirited, romantic, hopeful.*

Setting

Dover, Kentucky. On the Ohio River.
Scene One – Ripley, Ohio (Fall, 1905). Scene Two – Ohio.
River (Fall, 1863).
Scene Three – Dover, Kentucky (Fall, 1853).

Time

1853–1905.

Author's Note

The play takes place in a parlor (or living room) that transforms from scene to scene. The staging of it suggests some intricate elements, but the trick is to keep it simplistic. It's a ghost story, so much like a spirit, it needs only the impression of these elements. For the second scene, Arnold Gragston could be standing on a chair with a long wooden rod to simulate the ferryboat, as Edgar Bell sits on additional chair below him.

There is also a field holler throughout the play, usually used to call farm animals in from grazing. In the play it is used to create an eerie feeling, as if it is a call from the beyond. I imagine it to be long and wispy. I imagine the play darkly lit.

The Weatherin': A Ghost Play *by Jonathan Payne*

"Heathcliff, if I dare you now, will you venture? If you do, I'll keep you. I'll not lie there by myself: they may bury me twelve feet deep, and throw the church down over me, but I won't rest till you are with me. I never will!"

Emily Brontë, Wuthering Heights

Pitch black.

At the height of expectancy it happens.

A loud and raucous banging on a door.

A face out of the darkness appears.

It's Fall, 1905. **Edgar***, seated in a waning parlor, listens for a moment.*

Edgar   Hear that?

He waits.

Course you don't . . . Folks ain't got ears, less it's in front of 'em. Most got eyes, won't see . . .

A call is heard in the distance.

Ah . . . you hear it.

The call grows in intensity. It is the call of a lady of the fields, and it fills the space with a longing desperation. It is slow and deliberate.

Emily (*offstage*)   EE-YI-HOO, EE-YI-HOO, OO-HEEH, OO-HEEH, HALLIE, COME ON!

He continues to listen, and then:

Edgar   Sperits? You wanna know 'bout the power people tells you I has. I scairt of them. I can always tell when sperits is roun'. Got a queer scent. They fulled up—got too much *feelin'*. No where's to put it! I'm used to 'em. But they'll devil you, too. They don't do nothin' to me; only talk at me. How I learnt such? It am forty years ago or so now when I first fully realize that I has de power. Lef' my wife on the plantation. Took a boat 'cross the Ohi'an river to freedom.

That's when I first saw her . . . or it – Her . . . Then I knew. History's a ghost we just love to ignore . . . It'll remind ya, though. One time to another, my time to your time . . . Forty years ago it was. Night I cross that river . . . somebody died . . .

There's a loud raucous banging on a door.

Arnold *is revealed, standing at the bow of a tiny boat, steering* **Edgar** *down a river.*

It's Fall, 1863. It's raining.

Arnold   There's s'posed to be two of ya'.

Edgar   I tole you she ain't comin'.

Arnold   She ya wife.

Edgar   She was too scared to come.

Arnold   You s'posed to be her backbone.

Edgar   She was too scared, I said. How I force that woman to do anything? Keep mentionin' me love. I got duties to her. But it ain't no true love. Ain't no nigga South of Ohio talkin' love—

Arnold   I only out here once an' again! When the moon got it's back to us, s'posed to take as many as I can.

Edgar   Calm ya'self! I'se scared enough. You been the devil all night. I gets ya! Now I 'ppreciates ya takin me 'cross this here river. You done save my life . . .

Arnold   Coulda saved another.

Edgar   Oh, alright . . . (*Long beat.*) How you come to do this?

Arnold (*sharply*)   Regret. Regrets brought me to this river. Somethin' I shoulda done a time ago.

Edgar   Why you say it to me like that? All 'cusitory like.

Arnold   Maybe I been where you been.

Edgar   You been where I been? Sure you been in my toes you do the same damn thing. I hear slaves a chatterin' 'bout this here boat on the Ohio, no way I miss it. A slave grow a foot taller in the North. That's, that.

The boat dips.

Arnold   Hol' on now . . .

Edgar   River's lively . . . How you know where we goin' anyway? Rain's bad enough. Cain't see past my nose.

Arnold   There's a light down yonder. See it?

Edgar   So we headin' to the light.

Arnold   Yes'suh.

Edgar   Headin' to the light. That's funny. I prays for I come here. Iffen my ma hear me talk Jesus. She was a "Conger," and they was all scared of her. Couldn't give her the Bible . . .

Arnold   That so.

Edgar   Folk tie her up, they forget to whip her.

Arnold   You foolin'.

Edgar   I ain't no lie. A conger she was. Had whites doin' what she want.

Arnold   Storytellin'.

Edgar   There things can't be explained.

Arnold   You eatin' your fingers.

Edgar   Guessin' I'm scared. Feels sick . . .

Arnold   Moon's gone. It's a black night. No one lookin' for slaves out here.

Edgar   It's the ghost that scares me, 'sides the runnin' . . .

Arnold   Ain't been caught yet. Folks cross the river got it planned.

Edgar   You hear me, ain't ya?

Arnold   What?

Edgar   The ghost. (*Beat.*) Is it truth? I hear talk there's a spirit in this here river.

Arnold   What I hear. Ain' seen her yet. Been on this river 'long time.

Edgar   She a angry spirit. She was in love, with the wrong man, what I hear. Her massa takes a big long knife and cuts her head plumb off.

Arnold   I hear—

Edgar   Ties a great, heavy weight to her, and makes her lover toss her in this here river.

Arnold   I hear, I said.

Edgar   She only come durin' the weatherin'. You hear her callin' in the night—

Arnold (*suddenly angry*)   You hush that nonsense! I 'cross this river a year, ain' seen nothin' yet!

Edgar *stands.*

Edgar   I'm tired of your mouth, mister! Don't know why you so vex—

Arnold   SIT . . . DOWN . . . You knock this boat over . . . We gonna fall in!

He forces **Edgar** *back down.*

Edgar   Boat to freedom. 'Spectin' somebody more friendly.

Arnold   What you say?

Edgar   You hear that?

Arnold   Hear what?

Edgar *strains to listen.* **Arnold** *is oddly interested.*

Arnold   What you hearin'?

Edgar   Listen.

A few minutes pass.

Arnold   Rain on the water, all it is.

Edgar   Don't . . . know . . .

Arnold   Maybe it your wife come to fix ya.

Edgar   I lef' her. All there is, is me. Me, now. That's that.

Arnold   You guilty!

Edgar   Guilt last as long as you think on it.

Voice (*offstage*) (*chanted through the rest of the scene*)   EE-YI-HOO, EE-YI-HOO, OO-HEEH, OO-HEEH, HALLIE, COME ON!

A figure appears from far off.

Edgar   Hear that?

Arnold   Yeah! Yeah I do!

Edgar   Water's risin'!

Arnold   Lord . . . in . . . heaven . . .

Edgar   The weatherin' done picked up!

After a few moments.

Look there! I sees her. She's . . . there . . .

Arnold   EMILY! I sees ya! I sees ya! Take me with ya, I'm ready now!

Edgar   What you talkin'?

Arnold   Forgive me—

Edgar   You gonna knock this boat—

Arnold   I'm ready now!

Edgar   She's comin' . . .

Arnold   Forgive me! I'm ready!

Edgar   She comin' cross the water!

Before they can utter another word, there's a loud crash, a flash of light, and the boat capsizes, throwing the men into the swelling river.

Blackout.

A loud and raucous knocking on a door.

Lights up on **Arnold**'s *slave quarters.*

Emily *enters. It's the Fall, 1853.*

Arnold   You're soaked to the bone.

Emily   It's rainin' wild. (*Beat.*) I come to ask ya to leave.

Arnold   You married now. Best leave my quarters.

Emily   Arnold, there's a woman who helps folk up the Ohio to freedom. Let's leave here.

Arnold   You found here, you'll end up in the river.

Emily   My husb—he don't know I'm here. (*Beat.*) He sleep. On the floor. "You's teched in the head," I tol'em. He tryin' to sleep with me. So's I puts my feet 'gainst him and give him a shove and out he go on the floor. Dat nigga jump up and he mad. He look like de wild bear—

Arnold   I ain't runnin', Emily. You hear what he done to runners when he catch 'em.

Emily   You got to come with me—

Arnold   He fill the Ohi'an he would.

Emily   We can make it! I know we can.

Arnold   *You* got to leave!

He checks the window.

Stormin' outside, cain't see a thing. Please, Emily.

He places a blanket around her shoulders.

You take this. Get on back to your . . . husband!

Emily   I brought the book.

Arnold   Emily. Cain't be doin' this now!

Emily   The poems we been sharin'—

Arnold   Emily!

Emily   We the only people 'wake in this world.

Arnold   Don't start in on that.

Emily   Them words you read me. I got them with me—

Arnold   Things different now.

Emily   Ain't nothin' done changed. I still love—

Arnold   Don't say that now. That word stay nowhere round here!

Emily   You tol'me such.

Arnold   Then I don't know what it means. (*Beat.*) You can't be comin' 'round here that word comin' out your mouth! That word don't belong to nobody like us!

Emily   Then who it belong to?

Arnold   Don't know. I'm made for plowin', and you made for tendin' animals!

Emily   Thought love and freedom don't know what death is. You say it's the stubborn rock.

Arnold   That's just storytellin'.

Emily   Then what *we* mean, Arnold? That just storytellin' to you?

Arnold   . . . Emily . . .

Emily   You scared is what you is! Coward! A big ol' fool of a—

There's a loud raucous banging on the door.

Arnold   Look what you done—Tail it out the back!

More banging, slowly increasing.

Emily (*beat.*)   Either we leave or he kill us.

Arnold   Go on out the back . . .

More pounding. **Arnold** *stands against the door.*

Emily   We both be sperits.

Arnold   Emily, please.

Emily   Let 'em come on, then.

Arnold   You gots to stop this!

Emily   Love is the stubborn rock is what you tol' me.

Arnold   I lied to ya! I lied . . . *Please* go . . .

Emily   Come in! Come in!

Arnold   Emily—

Emily   Come on in! You hear me—

The door is forced open. The storm blows out the candle light.

The chant is all that remains.

EE-YI-HOO, EE-YI-HOO, OO-HEEH, OO-HEEH, HALLIE, COME ON!

Play #22: Slow Gin Fits *by Angelica Chéri*

In a spirited game of gin rummy, Harold and Dinah discover they are both in need of a little more than a card game and small talk to pass the time and kill the pain.

Wonder what a little liquid courage can do? Presented in The Fire This Time Festival Season 5, directed by Cezar Williams, performed by Toccara Cash (**Dinah**) and Leopold Lowe (**Harold**).

Slow Gin Fits: A Short Play *by Angelica Chéri*

The living room of a well-kept apartment with a feminine touch. Fictional Chicago, circa 1945.

Lights come up on **Dinah** *(late twenties/early thirties, demure) and* **Harold** *(late thirties, rustic, charming) sitting on the couch, in the middle of a card game.*

Dinah   Discard already, Mr. Virgil, my gray hairs have gray hairs.

Harold   Ain't no gray hair on your whole head.

Dinah   Will be by the time you take your turn.

Harold   Patience, woman.

Dinah   What you holdin' in there, the Queen of England?

Harold   I never shows my hand.

Dinah   Let me see.

Harold   Unh-uh. No peekin', little girl.

Dinah   I ain't no little girl.

Harold   You as green as a blade'a grass.

Dinah   You feelin' froggy, go ahead and leap then.

Harold   Shhhhhhhh.

Dinah   Leap, baby. Come on with it.

Harold *scratches his head, and finally puts a card down.*

Harold   Good Jack don't crack.

Dinah *stares blankly at the card pile.*

Dinah   Mr. Virgil, I think you might have taken the cake on this one.

Harold   I always gets my slice.

Dinah   That right?

Harold   Sho 'nuff.

Dinah   Tell you what . . .

She puts a card down

Go ahead and sink your teeth into that.

Harold*'s face falls in disbelief.*

Dinah   Sweet ain't it? Ha ha ha!

Harold   You was holdin' a king?! The whole time?

Dinah   I never shows my hand.

Harold   You cheatin'!

Dinah   How I'm cheatin'?

Harold   Ain't no woman *ever* beat me in no gin rummy.

Dinah   Guess it's a first time for everything, ain't it?

Harold   You too much, baby girl, too much.

Dinah   Not too much, just enough.

Harold   Playin' cards, talkin' trash . . . betcha yo daddy don't know nothin' 'bout these little hobbies of yours, do he?

Dinah   Sho' don't. Neither do he know his head usher is over at his daughter's house, unsupervised at ten o'clock on a Saturday night. Do he, Mr. Virgil?

Harold   Call me Harold.

He leans into **Dinah** *for a kiss. She leans in as well. The loud ding of a kitchen timer interrupts them.*

Dinah   My muffins!

She jumps up and rushes to the kitchen. Beat.

Harold *checks his breath. Unsatisfied, he reaches into his pocket for a tube of Binaca, and gives himself a spritz.*

Then he goes into his bag and produces a bottle of gin and two paper cups. He pours.

Dinah *re-enters with two muffins on a plate.*

Dinah   My famous blueberry pecan muffins, hot and fresh out the ahhh–

She quivers in pain as she sets the muffins down, almost dropping them.

Harold   Baby girl!

Dinah   Oooooo, Jesus.

Harold   You alright?

Beat as **Dinah** *tries desperately to recover.*

Dinah   I'm fine . . . Just a little shootin' pain, comes and goes.

Harold   You sho'? I know a doctor, lives right up Kincaid Street.

Dinah   I'm alright, I'm alright.

Harold   You need you a lil taste.

He offers her a cup of gin.

Dinah   What in the world is that?

Harold   What in the world is what?

Dinah   That—swill.

Harold   Ain't no swill, woman. This is genuine, full-body Seagram's gin.

Dinah   I don't drink no gin!

Harold   You don't?

Dinah   I don't drink period.

Harold   Then what in the world did you mean when you said, "Why don't you come on over tonight, Mr. Virgil, and have a little gin"?

Dinah   I said *play* a little gin.

Harold   No you didn't.

Dinah   You tellin' me what I said?

Harold   I know what I heard.

Dinah   You heard what you wanted to hear.

Harold   Well, this ain't 'bout to go to waste. This good gin right here.

He takes a swig of his gin. He offers the other cup to **Dinah***, but she refuses.*

Harold   Come on now, you know I don't like drinkin' alone.

Dinah   Dizzy Grady's is open. Right on up the street.

Harold   I ain't tryna be up in Dizzy's with them winos.

Dinah   Like you ain't one of 'em.

Harold   Come on, baby, just a lil sip.

Dinah   No, sir. I don't even like the way it smell.

Harold   Smell like heaven in glass. Like sweat just a rollin' off a Jesus' eyebrows.

Dinah   You goin' to hell.

Harold   See, that's what's wrong with all y'all. Always tryna to send somebody to hell. Like you collecting rent from the devil. It ain't gonna kill you to get yourself a little taste of the moon every once in a while. Drop a little oil off in your flame. Loosen up your girdle and taste the good air.

Beat.

Dinah　I don't wear no girdle.

Harold *takes a big swig.*

Harold　Whew! Hit me right in the back. Got me feelin' like a new man. Look at that.

He takes a hearty stretch backward.

Dinah　You got a bad back?

Harold　Not right now I don't. Ol' Ginny here is my number one painkiller.

He takes another swig and takes a deep stretch forward and backward.

Look at that. I ain't been able to move like that in years. Wrenched my back fightin' fires three summers ago.

They said if I couldn't get it together I was gonna hafta hang up my hose. Couldn't do that, got a house to pay for. Took a swig of this here sunshine one mornin', and my back was as good as new.

Dinah *watches as* **Harold** *continues stretching.*

Dinah　You mean you don't feel no kinda pain?

Harold　Not a drop.

He slides the other cup to **Dinah**.

She contemplates, and then sips the cup dry.

Duke Ellington's "Prelude to a Kiss" enters overhead as **Dinah** *stands up tall and reaches all the way forward. She dangles her arms.*

Dinah　You right . . . you right. I ain't got no pain! Ain't no pain at all!

Harold　Tried to tell you, baby girl. You brand new now.

Dinah　I done forgot what pain-free felt like.

She twirls her arms and glides like a dancer.

Harold *pulls her in and they dance closely, rejoicing in their newly pain-free bodies.*

Their eyes meet. **Harold** *strokes* **Dinah**'s *cheek and kisses her passionately. The kiss escalates.*

Harold *lifts* **Dinah** *off the floor, wrapping her legs around his back. He carries her to the couch and removes his shirt. He tries to remove hers, but she jerks him away. "Prelude to a Kiss" exits.*

Harold　What? What's the matter?

Silence.

Harold   Come on now, why you clam up on me?

Dinah   You should go home, Mr. Virgil.

Harold   I do something wrong?

Dinah   No . . .

Harold   I ain't mean to come on so strong. Just thought we was feelin' the same way.

Dinah   It did feel mighty nice . . .

Harold   Ol' Ginny make the pain the go away, baby girl.

Dinah   The pain . . . But not everything.

She turns to **Harold** *and removes her shirt to reveal one breast intact, and the left side of her chest completely bandaged up.*

Dinah   I'm only half a woman, Mr. Virgil . . . They had to cut my other half off before it killed me. Said I oughta be grateful. Grateful to still be breathing . . . The Cancer been knocking on my family's door for generations. My grandmama called it that. "The Cancer." Like it was somebody. A crooked man that kept takin' ladies out on the town, never bringin' 'em back home. Took Grandmama for a dance. Took Mama out for a dance. And then me. Took me out dancing on a cold hospital table for weeks. Hollowed me out with a silver spoon like a grapefruit. Then sent me back home, in halves . . . So g'on ahead and go home, Mr. Virgil. Know you ain't got no use for half a woman.

Beat.

Harold *lifts* **Dinah***'s fallen chin with his hand.*

Harold   I done told you, call me Harold.

He wraps his arms around her and kisses her forehead gently. Her fears melt away in his chest.

Play #23: Love and Happiness: Ada's Story
by Fredrica Bailey

Set in 1939 against the vibrant, vivacious backdrop of juke joints and jazzy blues, this play centers on a middle-aged Black woman in love with a much younger man. With a secret to tell and a decision to make she grapples with age, love, and the realities of life.

Presented in The Fire This Time Festival Season 8, directed by Cezar Williams, performed by Sidiki Fofana (**Hershel Tyes**), Patrice Bell (**Charlene**) and Karen Chilton (**Ada Baker**).

Characters

Ada Baker, *forty, African American woman. Waitress at Miss Etta's Place.*
Hershel Tyes, *twenty-four, African American man. Clarinet player at Miss Etta's Place.*
Charlene, *twenty-five, African American woman. Waitress at Miss Etta's Place.*

Love and Happiness: Ada's Story—A Ten-Minute Play *by Fredrica Bailey*

Scene One

1939—The woods. A small shack in the middle of nowhere. Music blaring out the windows. The sound of horns, drumming, and singing saturate the air. Every crevice, nook, and cranny oozes jazzy blues.

Sign outside reads "Miss Etta's Place."

Inside **Ada**, *forty, short, chubby, and brown, walks through the crowded spot to the bar. She carries with her a tray of empty glasses.*

She spots **Charlene**, *twenty-five, approaching. She leans against the bar waiting and staring at a Black and white couple in the corner.*

Charlene   Woo wee, Ada! It's on fire in here tonight! You see these flo'boards creakin'! We fittin' to fall through this floor!

She does a little dance, twirling her bar rag as she stomps to the rhythm of the music.

Ada (*to* **Charlene**)   Hmph. Somethin' on fire, alright. You see that white girl over there with Perry Jackson? Goin' to be a world of trouble. She probably already got one in that oven.

Charlene *fills* **Ada**'s *tray with new drinks.* **Ada** *picks one up as if about to drink it herself.*

Charlene   Well, if you ask me you ain't got no time to be worried bout them. Not with that one you totin'.

Ada *rolls her eyes as* **Charlene** *snatches the drink from her hand, placing it back on the serving tray.*

Ada   Alright now, Charlene. I ain't tell ya for you to be throwin' it up at me every chance ya get. I'll be taking care of it soon anyway . . . I know someone.

Charlene   Who? Belle? Girl, you crazy! That woman ain't nothing but a witch doctor.

Ada   Well, what you suggest I do? Huh?! I don't know if I want no baby. Kinda like things the way they is.

She taps her feet to the music and starts to shimmy.

Charlene   Well, maybe I'm stickin' my nose somewhere it don't belong . . .

Ada (*nodding her head in agreement*)   Maybe.

Ada *goes for another drink.* **Charlene** *catches her hand mid-air . . .*

Charlene   But! If it was me, I'd at least tell the baby's father.

Staring at the band's clarinet player.

Especially when he a fine, dark, lean, tall, drink of—

Ada   'Scuse you! . . . Anyway, what if I don't know who the father is?

Charlene   What? Girl, you's know who he is. We all know. Ain't been able to keep your eyes or hands off 'em since he came to town.

Staring at the clarinet player again.

And you know what? I. Don't. Blame. You!

Ada   Charlene!

Charlene   What?! Oh! Point is he a good man, Ada. So I don't see why—

Ada   He a boy! I don't know what I was thinking. Here I am forty years old, unmarried, in the later part of life. And pregnant! He'd be better off with someone like, like you.

Charlene   He ain't pick me! And jus cause he young, don't mean he ain't a man. You should talk to him, come on now, after closin'.

Ada *stares at the band as they play. She looks at* **Hershel***, twenty-four, the young clarinet player. He winks at her.*

Charlene   'Sides, you sho' don't look at him like he a boy.

Ada   Hush up, you ol' fresh thing!

Charlene (*smiling and giggling*)   So, is you going to do it? Is ya? Is ya?

Ada *picks up another drink, but this time puts it down herself.*

Ada   Alright . . . Boy goin' drop dead sho' nuff though. Clarinet and all.

Later, Miss Etta's is closing. Stragglers are about, but **Ada** *pretends to be busy cleaning up. When she finds neither* **Charlene** *or* **Hershel** *looking, she puts down her broom and slips out the back door.*

She hurries down a dirt path and is only a couple hundred or so feet away, when **Hershel** *calls out and comes running over. The two talk while walking.*

Hershel   I see you come out the back this time.

Ada   That's right, Hershel. I's real busy, gots to get going this evening.

Hershel   I was waiting for you, is all.

Ada   Well . . . here I am.

Hershel   So, you mind if I walk with you like usual?

Ada   Suit yourself.

For a moment **Ada** *and* **Hershel** *walk in silence. The moon hangs huge and bright above them. And the stars, so clear and shiny look ripe for picking. Little lightning bugs light the path ahead of them.*

Hershel   Ain't that beautiful?

Ada   What?

Hershel   Listen.

The insects in the forest and bush play a beautiful tune in perfect harmony with one another.

Hershel   Sounds like a symphony. Way better than anything man can make up if you ask me.

Ada   What you mean?! Those crickets?! Boy—

Hershel   Look, just be still a minute.

He holds **Ada** *still in front of him and stands behind her.*

Hershel (*whispering in her ear*)   Just listen.

For a split moment **Ada** *decides not to fight it and she hears what* **Hershel** *hears. It is beautiful. She starts to smile but then catches herself, abruptly clearing her throat and walking on.*

Ada   All I hear is these creaky old legs of mine.

Hershel   Come on, now. I like every dimple, valley, and hill on those legs. And we both knows they ain't creaky.

Ada *turns beat red.*

Ada   Boy, hush.

Hershel   I think they beautiful. I think you's beautiful, Miss Ada.

Ada   Oh God, "Miss."

Hershel   Would you let me call you . . . "Ada"? Even in our alone moments I usually call ya "Miss."

Ada   Go 'head with all this foolishness.

Hershel (*smiling*)   Let me try it out. (*Singing.*) Adaaaa. Adaaaa.

Ada *begins to fidget and smile again, despite herself.*

Ada   On second thought "Miss" may be better. Leave it to you to do too much!

Hershel   Why you so scared, Ada? Age make that much a difference to ya?

Ada   It's sixteen years, Hershel. Ain't nothing to sneeze at. You deserve somebody young, full of life . . . beautiful.

Hershel   You're right.

Ada (*frowning*)   I am?

Hershel   Of course. That's why I got you.

Ada   No, you don't understand. I mean a nice innocent girl. I ain't young like I use to be. And I done seen some things. Done did some things too.

Hershel   I certainly hope so. I aims for a woman that's lived a little and that's ready to keep on living. Life's too short for all these rules.

Ada   Point is, Hershel, you's too young to be saddled down with an old lady like me. I want you to go on and leave me alone. You live your life as best you can. And I wish you only good things, okay? You a good man. And you sho' deserve it.

Hershel *grabs her hand.*

Hershel   I'm sorry to tell you, Ada Baker, but you don't know what's best for me. I do. And I wants you.

Ada   Hershel, just stop! I'm pregnant! Okay?! There I said it! You see what I mean?!

Hershel *jumps up in the air clapping and smacking his hands together.*

Hershel   Hot dog!

Ada   What?!

Hershel   Baby, that's what got you talking like this? It mine ain't it?!

Ada *whips around, hitting him with her purse.*

Ada   Yes, it yours!

Hershel (*laughing*)   I'm just foolin' ya.

Ada   This is very serious, Hershel. Now I don't want you to think I expect anything of ya. You's young and you can go on with your life. I'll handle the—

Hershel *drops to one knee amidst the woods.*

Ada   Hershel?! Hershel! What you doing?!

Hershel   Ada Baker, here among the moon, the stars, and all the crickets, will you marry me?

Ada*'s breath catches in her chest for a moment. She holds back tears.*

Ada .   See! Now that's the youngest thing I ever did hear. Moons and crickets and such! And no! You don't have to do that just cause I'm in a way. I don't need nobody's pity.

Hershel   It ain't like that, baby. I promise. Look here, look here.

He pulls out a ring and holds it up to her. She won't touch it.

Read it, baby. Read the inside.

Ada *carefully takes it. She reads aloud.*

Ada   To my soon to be wife . . . Ada, from Hershel.

She looks down at him still on one knee, shocked. She begins to cry.

Ada   But how—how did you know?

Hershel   About the baby?—Didn't. Got this after the first time I walked you home.

Ada   So you was going to give this to me anyway? With or without the baby, I mean?

Hershel   You don't know by now? I love you, Ada Baker. So, that a yes? Say yes, mama.

Ada *stares at him on one knee. Young, but committed, determined.*

Ada   Yes.

Hershel *springs to his feet. He places the ring on her finger and swings her around. The two kiss.*

Hershel   Now, once you have the baby we'll move to New York. And I'll—

Ada   New York?! I ain't going to no New York, Hershel!

Hershel   Well, I ain't going without ya. That's where all the great musicians have to go to make their mark. And I don't know if you noticed, but can't nobody make that clarinet sing like Hershel Tyes.

Ada   But got my job, here. Miss Etta's.

Hershel   Come on, girl, we in it together now.

Ada *frowns.* **Hershel** *squeezes her waist a couple of times, trying to bring her around.*

Hershel   I can make some real money. Take care of us right. You rollin' with your young ol' man or not? Either together or not at all.

Ada *begins to crack a smile.*

Ada   Yeah, I'm rolling with my young ol' man.

Hershel (*excited*)   That's my girl! So when you be ready to leave?

Ada *hesitates.*

Ada   Soon. Ain't got no family. So just—just have to tell Charlene. And then stop by and see my friend . . . Belle.

Hershel   Alright then!

Ada *looks at him with a mixture of happiness and sadness.* **Hershel***, none the wiser, is still over the moon.*

They finally step out onto the main road, hand in hand. **Hershel** *hums a little tune as they walk the empty road together.*

Play #24: Gravity *by Josh Wilder*

Two men/made of clay/discover their wings.

Presented in The Fire This Time Festival Season 5, directed by Reginald Douglas, performed by Larry Powell (**Clay**) and Segun Akande (**Clay**).

Gravity: A Physical Awakening *by Josh Wilder*

Dedicated to the new angels in America; known and unknown.

A living room with cloud-painted walls; the floor is the color of a starry night. Two men covered in clay, both contrasting colors, stand on a white mattress facing each other.

Clayman 1/Clayman 2

Every time I make a connection with somebody—like if I put all the guys I had a connection with in one soul that would be the guy for me. Maybe I need to get older to fully realize that, but I'm getting there.

Where you going?

To find fulfillment.

Fulfillment. [?]

Yeah he looks just like you but a little taller.

You gonna be addicted to finding him cause he don't exist.

That's okay I'll keep looking.

You don't want love?

I do.

I'll love you.

I just met you.

But still I'll love you.

You look like love.

That's all I ever wanted, but I fulfillment is always signing off.

Ignoring you?

Like you're never gonna be tall enough?

Skinny enough?

Cut enough?

Cute enough?

Long enough?

Thick enough?

Enough?

So . . .

Yeah . . .

You an angel?

I'm clay.

Yeah, but angels were molded from something. That's not me.

Me neither.

Okay.

Okay.

Then . . .

So . . .

Yes!

Energy!

Strength!

Passion!

Where were you all this time? I dunno I just came in.

Don't come out. Unlock it. Unlock yours! It's open.

You mind?

It's open.

My body!

Our bodies flying!

Colliding.

Glaciers melting.

Chakras becoming one big circle. Blood rushing.

Breath taking me . . . UUUUUUUUUUH!!!!!!!!!!!!!!!!! Gravity.

. . . . Gravity

They collide, mixing tones, dirtying the white bed.

I see you still.

What are you thinking about?

Tomorrow.

Tomorrow.

Yeah, is your face gonna show tomorrow. I dunno.

There goes fulfillment—

I—

I know he ain't real I just had a thought.

You think. You get hurt.

You don't think the hurt is worse.

Can you pretend that you love me?

?

Just until the sun rises then you can fly away.

What if I like it? What if I want to stay until the moon? You're not supposed to be real, right?

Pretend love.

Lust disguised as unequal love with a fulfillment mask. That's fine.

They fall on the bed. Beat.

I love you.

I love you now. Tomor—

NOW!

Fly with me. Ok.

How?

Jump!

They begin to jump on the mattress.

They roll around in the bed, switching off who's on top of who.

Reach for something! Jump!

hahaahhha

I'm flying

This

You are fulfillment

You teaching me how to fly You teaching me how to love You . . .

Ah! What? Blood. Where? Sit down.

Turn.

Haha okay.

You.

What?

You.

What! I'm what? An angel.

Don't say that.

Why you say that? You have feathers. No I don't!

Look!

This ain't mine.

Clayman ___ *tries to hug* **Clayman** ___ *mid-jump and winces.*

Gravity takes them down.

Clayman ___ *removes some clay from his back and finds a feather. Beat.*

Beat.

It cut me. look . . . stand up.

Am I one now? Turn around.

He stands. They stand.

Clayman ___ *grabs into his back ripping out a hand full of feathers. Gravity takes them down.*

Wait.

Don't fall.

I'm an angel struck with gravity . . . you struck me with gravity! So me? Now it's me!?

It wasn't me!

Oh it was fulfillment?

It wasn't love!

Love expired when the jumping stopped . . .

They both are leaning with their backs against each other.

A baptism.

A conversion.

An invisible supernova.

Help me.

Help me up.

How do we fly against the gravity? Flap harder.

Pray stronger.

Love for real.

But only me more.

Yeah.

Fulfill me more with me.

We're angels now? Flying secretly. Or proudly

Beat.

Or knowingly

That others might clip our wings.

Play #25: Maya and Rivers *by Tyler English-Beckwith*

Maya and Rivers are from a dead earth in search of a new life. They find it together, on the moon.

Presented in The Fire This Time Festival Season 11, directed by Ebony Noelle Golden, performed by Linda LaBeija (**Moon Maya**), Trevor Latez Hayes (**Rivers**), and Paris Cymone (**Earth Maya**).

Characters

Moon Maya, *Black. Late teens to early twenties.*
Earth Maya, *Black. Late teens to early twenties.*
Rivers, *Black. Early twenties.*

Maya and Rivers *by Tyler English-Beckwith*

Moon Maya *is the past. She is the Milky Way. She is vast and wide.*

Earth Maya *is present. She is not older, but wiser. Still vast and wide, but rocky.*

Rivers *is the beautiful and fading faster than he thinks.*

Earth Maya *is not in the world of* **Moon Maya** *and* **Rivers**. *She can no longer breathe in their atmosphere. She watches, speaking to us.*

Earth Maya   Do you know how many stars there are? I don't. I've never tried to count them either. I had never told someone I loved them more than all of the stars in the sky because I don't know how many there are. I don't know how many stars are stuck up in that vast black space so how could I measure something like love, to something I've never been sure of? I had never told someone I loved them more than all of the stars in the sky until . . .

Air.

Earth Maya   "Ain't No Sunshine" was my favorite song that summer. I sang it everywhere: school, shower, work, moon. We went to the moon and I taught it to him there. He was always horrible at learning tunes but this one stuck, and boy he sang it on every trip. He was so funny out there. It was like the atmospheric pressure of earth was preventing him from having a sense of humor. But on the moon he was my favorite comedian.

Rivers   Who earns a living driving their customers away? TAXI DRIVERS!

Moon Maya *is stone faced, but soon she melts.*

Earth Maya   Even the corny ones were funny. We just sat in a crater eating tootsie rolls singing that song and laughing. I had never laughed so much. One time, he was doing back flips and his hat fell right off his head. It almost looked like it was headed toward our neighborhood . It would have been so perfect had it landed right on his front porch.

Perfect.

Air.

Earth Maya   The water plant was shutting down, and so was our world. The old heads remembered when water rushed past their feet and people didn't gawk at the phenomenon, it just was. That's what he was named after, the body of water forever flowing forward, Rivers. His name was Rivers.

Rivers   I wish we could stay here forever.

Moon Maya   How many orbs do we have left? I don't want to run out of time.

Rivers   We're in space and you're worried about time.

Moon Maya   We have to get back soon.

Rivers   Dance with me, my Maya. Dance with me on the moon. Maybe we could . . . moonwalk!

They laugh together.

Rivers *glides across the surface of the moon.*

Moon Maya *attempts, but she isn't as smooth as* **Rivers**. *He walks behind her and places his hands in the curve of her waist.*

Rivers   Not from here.

She delights at his touch, but she's sure to covert.

Rivers   You don't want to wine. It's not about the feet either. I mean it is, like you do have to glide or whatever. But the trick is the shoulders.

Rivers *moves* **Moon Maya**'s *braids in front of her. He rubs her shoulders, moving them in a circular motion.*

Rivers   It's about the illusion.

He moves beside her and moves his shoulders along with her. He adds it all together perfectly. **Moon Maya** *attempts, but it's not quite there.*

Moon Maya   I'm not good at it.

Rivers   You don't have to be.

Light air.

Rivers   I've got enough rhythm for the both of us.

He hits a spin move, but he loses his balance.

Moon Maya   Be careful. What would I do if I lost you out here?

Rivers   You'd go back home and burn baby burn in that dry ass heat. Its like we're closer to the sun down there than we are up here. I feel like I'm boiling at home, but this. Who knew that a lack of oxygen could be so refreshing?

Moon Maya   Lack of oxygen? How many orbs?

Rivers   Enough for twenty more tootsie rolls.

Moon Maya   Five more.

Rivers   Ten.

Moon Maya (*deep sigh*)   Ok. Ten.

Moon Maya *takes a handful of tootsie rolls out of her pocket and hands* **Rivers** *half.*

Moon Maya (*rapping*)   Cotton candy. Sweet 'n' low.

Rivers   Let me see you tootsie roll!
Ayyyye!

Moon Maya   Ayyyye!

Rivers

They both break out into the tootsie roll. This time **Moon Maya** *is better and* **Rivers** *is goofy.*

He watches her enjoy herself for a moment. She stops when she realizes.

Rivers   Uh huh. You're all about rolling them hips.

He imitates her sexy roll. They laugh.

Moon Maya   Staaahhhp.

Rivers (*mocking*)   Staaahhhp.

Moon Maya *blushes.*

Moon Maya   The last time we were up here I almost got caught. My mama heard me sneaking back in.

Rivers   Y'all still haven't gotten that screen door fixed?

Moon Maya   Nope. My daddy said it's a free alarm system.

Rivers   She get on you?

Moon Maya   I made up some lie about going to the plant to get fresh water, but I couldn't tell if she believed me or not. My daddy was at the launch pad so he didn't care. Third craft left yesterday. Fifty on board.

Rivers   Landing?

Moon Maya *shakes her head.*

Moon Maya   No survivors.

Rivers   I think a boy I knew in second grade was on that spacecraft. Joey. He had the biggest glasses I've ever seen on a person that small. Wanted to be a firefighter when he grew up.

Moon Maya   What did you want to be?

Rivers   I don't remember.

Moon Maya   You remember everything. You remembered the time I got my head stuck in between the banisters at your ninth birthday party.

Rivers   Well, that was hard to forget.

Moon Maya   Tell me.

Rivers   I wanted to be a rocket ship.

Moon Maya   A what?

Rivers   See naw. Uhn uhn.

He unwraps a tootsie roll and stuffs it in her mouth.

Moon Maya   I'm sorry I didn't mean to–

She stifles a laugh.

Rivers   Forget it.

Moon Maya *touches his arm lovingly.*

Moon Maya   Why a rocket ship?

Rivers *looks to* **Moon Maya** *for safety. She gives it to him.*

Rivers   Because then the fire would be under me. Not on top of me beating me down. It would lift me all the way up. I would be invincible. Unbreakable.

They share a smile. Air.

And you?

Moon Maya   I haven't really though about it.

Rivers   Yeah right. You think about everything.

Moon Maya   You promise not to judge?

Rivers   I just told you I wanted to be a rocket ship. No judgment here.

Moon Maya   But it isn't like cool or progressive or revolutionary . . .

Rivers *takes her hand.*

Rivers   No judgment.

Moon Maya   I want to be a mother.

Air.

You think it's stupid.

Rivers   No, of course not. But what about the mandatory contraception?

Moon Maya   It isn't realistic, Rivers. It's just . . . something I want, but I can't have. I want to create. We live in a world where nothing grows or flows organically. But a mother creates inside of her the greatest gift of all. Life. She nurtures it and guides it. The way Mother Luna used to guide the tides. She bestows it with all the energy she can manifest. On an earth with empty vessels, the greatest thing you can be is full.

Air.

I love you, Rivers.

Rivers   What?

Moon Maya   I love you, Rivers. More than there are stars in the sky, more than you love the moon, I love you.

Earth Maya   I love you, Rivers. More than there are stars in the sky, more than you love the moon, I love you.

Rivers   Don't say that.

Moon Maya   Why?

Rivers   There's no time for love. No place for it.

Moon Maya   But, I do.

Rivers *looks at his oxygen pack.*

Rivers   Two orbs of oxygen left. Two orbs left up here in this perfect emptiness. Then we go back to a dead planet, and we pretend like we're living.

Don't waste these last moments on saying things that can never manifest, because in a world with a manufactured life source something like love just isn't authentic. All we have is right here. All we have are these last two orbs.

Moon Maya   Lie to me, Rivers. Tell me that you can pack up the moon in the your backpack and bring it to me. Tell me that we could create a home in a crater. Tell me that we could just leave it in the backyard and bounce on it when we're sad. Tell me we could hide it from the neighborhood kids so that no one would know our lunar secret, but when I tell you I love you more than there are stars in the sky–

Rivers   I'm leaving on the next one.

Moon Maya   What?

Rivers   I bought a ticket this morning. I'm leaving on the next space craft tomorrow.

Moon Maya   Why?

Rivers   Why not?

Moon Maya   Thirteen percent success rate! That's what they advertise on the radio. Thirteen percent! Like they're proud of themselves. Do you know what happened to Joey?

Rivers   He flew above that giant dead rock.

Moon Maya   And then he came crashing down.

Rivers   What kind of existence is the one at home? My mouth is so dry some nights I find my self enjoying the act of swallowing my spit. We're all dying, my Maya.

He tries to grab her hand, but she snatches it away.

Moon Maya   You're a coward, too afraid to look into the faces of the people who are dying of thirst. I'm drinking my spit too, Rivers, but I'm not running away.

Rivers   There is nothing there for me!

Earth Maya   The stars went dark. The moon fell out of the sky. It was the end of the world.

Moon Maya   What about me?

Rivers   I want to be a rocket ship, Maya. The fire that flames below me only burns what's left behind.

Moon Maya   Soon, the world won't exist, and neither will we. But when you're flying, past the earth, past us all don't forget gravity. Don't forget what held you close. Close to the ground. Close to me.

Rivers *looks at his oxygen pack.*

Rivers   Half an orb left.

He traces her fingers with his.

You could come with me. I can get another tick–

Moon Maya *shakes her head.* **Rivers** *nods, understanding.*

Rivers   Can we dance again? One last time.

Moon Maya *nods.*

He walks behind her and grabs her waist, taking her in.

Rivers   How do you feel, my Maya?

Moon Maya   Full.

Earth Maya   The plant shut down four weeks later. We ran out of water last night. Some of us are leaving on crafts in the morning. A few of us are dying in our beds. I have not decided yet, but either way I will evaporate. I haven't seen Rivers since that last dance in space. I couldn't make myself go to the launch pad to say goodbye, because we'd never have the moon again. He's soaring somewhere higher than high. I checked the status on the radio the day after he left. No landing. But I know he's up there, counting the stars. 1, 2, 3, 4, 5, 6, 7 . . .

IV. The Fire This Time Festival Creative Team

Kelley Nicole Girod, Founder, Executive Director
In addition to founding and serving as Executive Director of OBIE award-winning The Fire This Time Festival, Kelley Nicole Girod is an award-winning playwright (2021 Sundance IDP Grant Recipient, Atlantic Launch New Play Commission 2019, Sheen Center Fellow 2019, Stein and Liberace Fellow 2007, John Golden Fellow 2008) whose work has been developed/presented at Atlantic Theater Company, Sheen Center for Thought and Culture, The Fire This Time Festival, Harlem 9, Primary Stages, Project Y, Poetic Theater Productions, Classical Theater of Harlem, Frigid NYC, Planet Connections Theater Festival, The Field, and Dixon Place, and Stanford University's TAPS Program. She is a 2020 nominee of the prestigious Paul Robeson Award.

Kelley has also served as a guest lecturer at Yale School for Drama, Stanford University's Theater Department, and Cal State, Fullerton. She is a 2008 Graduate of Columbia's MFA Playwriting Program.

Cezar Williams, Artistic Director
Cezar Williams is an award-winning actor, director, and producer. Acting credits include *James and Annie*, written by Tony Award winner Warren Leight, at the Actor's Studio, Ensemble Theatre of Cincinnati (dir: D. Lynn Meyers) and the Williamstown Theatre Festival (dir: Jack Hofsiss), *Section 310*, as part of the 2014 Summer Shorts NYC Theatre Festival (dir: Fred Berner), *Thunder* as part of the 2007 New York International Theatre Festival (dir: Greg Allen), *Ascension* at The National Black Theatre Festival (dir: Petronia Paley), and *Yanagai! Yanagai!* at LA Mama (co-dir: Harold Dean James and Karen Oughtred). Television appearances include *Bull*, *Shades of Blue*, *Law and Order*, *The Enemy Within*, *Search Party*, *NYC 22*, *Blue Bloods*, and *What Would You Do?* He can be seen on demand and on Netflix in the movies *Bad Hurt* and *Hudson Tribes*. Directing credits include the Off-Broadway premiere of *Dancing on Eggshells* (Billie Holiday Theatre), *Till: A Musical* (American Theater Group), *SWEAT* by Lynn Nottage (SUNY Purchase), *The October Storm* (Hudson Stage Co.), *Crowndation: I Will Not Lie to David* (National Black Theatre), *The Hunting Season* (Planet Connections Festivity, Award for Best Direction), *You Wouldn't Expect* (American Bard Theater), *How to Be Safe* (The Dirty Blondes in rep at the Kraine Theater), directing all seven short plays in the eighth annual The Fire This Time Festival, *Free Will* (The Arthur Seelen Theatre), *Ghost Town* and *Tailypo* (Detroit NY Festival), *Lunchtime in Heaven* (48 hours in Harlem), *Nightfall* and *Slow Gin Fits* (The Fire This Time Festival 2013 and 2014).

Cezar is a graduate of New York University where he was a Martin Luther King Jr. Scholar. He is a member of the Stage Directors and Choreographers Society.

A.J. Muhammad, Associate Producer and Director of New Works Lab
A.J. Muhammad has a background in library public service, dramaturgy, and arts administration. He has collaborated with the director, educator, and activist Daniel Banks on various projects directed by Banks in the US and regionally over the past two

decades. As a dramaturg and research assistant A.J. has worked on productions ranging from indie theater to higher education. He is also a producer for CLASSIX, an initiative that was founded by Awoye Timpo in 2017 to expand the theater canon through an exploration of dramatic works by Black authors.

Julienne Hairston, Producer

Julienne Hairston was born in Kenitra, Morocco. She lives and writes in New Rochelle, New York. She received her BA in Creative Writing from Hunter College, NY. She was selected to participate in Hunter College's inaugural MFA in Playwriting with Tony Nominated Playwright Tina Howe. She has written for Our Men Productions and The Mission Herald. Her plays have been featured in Hunter's Playwrights festival; Project Y's Racey Play Festival; Obie Award-winning The Fire This Time Festival (season six); Project Y's Techno Plays; PJulienneroject Y's Parity Plays; NY Indie Theater Annual one-minute Play Festival; Project Y's Women in Theater Festival; Madness Theater Ten Minute Festival. Julienne was a member of Project Y's 2015–17 Playwright Group. She was commissioned to write for WIT The Hrosthwitha Project 2017. She was a contributing member with Athena Writes 2017 fellowship. In 2018 she became a company member playwright with NYMadness. She is the founder of Lift as You Climb, Inc, a theater company dedicated to inspire and lift African American children through the experience of live theater, in Westchester County, New York.

Erez Ziv, Managing Director

Erez Ziv is the Managing Artistic Director of FRIGID New York. He has joyfully dedicated over twenty years of his life to creating a theatrical home for up-and-coming theatermakers in NYC. He is the proud recipient of an OBIE Award, IT Award, NYTE Award, and Acker Award all for community support. He is very happy to have firmly established FRIGID's reputation in the downtown theater scene and internationally and to have created a well-respected organization that continues to uplift some of New York City's most innovative, talented, and hardworking theater artists.

His educational history includes University of Minnesota, Jewish Theological Seminary, and the University of Oxford. He is a licensed fireguard, sprinkler systems inspector, flame proofing supervisor, Central Park carriage driver, and wedding ceremony officiant.

Thankfully the world keeps providing him with both fresh and refined talent to let loose on NYC and the world.

Erez is also a father.

Permissions and Acknowledgements

Permissions contact

Title of Play	Playwright	Playwright Contact	Agent Contact
The Beyoncé Effect	Katori Hall		MFinkle@WMEAgency.com
Citizen Jane	Derek Lee McPhatter	derekmcphatter@gmail.com	
Vanna White Has Got to Die!	Antoinette Nwandu		rweiner@icmpartners.com
Hard Palate	Roger Q. Mason	rogerqmason@gmail.com	
Third Grade	Dominique Morrisseau		jmills@paradigmagency.com
scholarship babies	Francisca Da Silveira		Jamie.KayePhillips@unitedtalent.com
Poor Posturing	Tracey Conyer Lee		johnessay@gmail.com
The Fucking World and Everything in It	C.A. Johnson		aschwartz@paradigmagency.com
Black, White, & Blue	William Watkins	william.oliver.watkins@gmail.com	
Ain't No Mo'	Jordan E. Cooper		Kevin.lin@caa.com
Assumed Positions	Natyna Bean	natynabean@gmail.com	
Within Untainted Wombs	Dennis A. Allen II	dallen.champion@gmail.com	
Antepartum	Deneen Reynolds-Knott		susan@gurmanagency.com
Just Another Sunday in the Park	Bernard Tarver	bt11360@aol.com	
Panopticon	Cyrus Aaron	blackhoursinfo@gmail.com	
Exodus	Camille Darby	camille.darby@gmail.com	
The Sporting Life of Icarus Jones	Marcus Gardley		skw@wmeentertainment.com
The House	Charly Evon Simpson		aschwartz@paradigmagency.com
Sisterhood in the Time of the Apocalypse	Kendra Augustin	childofamerica@hotmail.com	

Title of Play	Playwright	Playwright Contact	Agent Contact
C.O.G.s	Samantha Godfrey	sg4896@nyu.edu	
The Weatherin'	Jonathan Payne		Jamie.KayePhillips@unitedtalent.com
Maya and Rivers	Tyler English-Beckwith		ally.shuster@caa.com
Love and Happiness	Fredrica Bailey		andrea.nelsonmeigs@unitedtalent.com
Slow Gin Fits	Angelica Chéri		BBlickers@apa-agency.com
Gravity	Josh Wilder	wilder.josh@gmail.com	